THE HAMLYN
BASIC GUIDE TO
WINEMAKING

HAMLYN

London · New York · Sydney · Toronto

Editor: Mary Lambert
Art Editors: Edward Pitcher, Andrea Ryan

Published by The Hamlyn Publishing Group Limited
London New York Sydney Toronto
Bridge House, 69 London Road, Twickenham, Middlesex TW1 3SB

Produced by Marshall Cavendish Books Limited
58 Old Compton Street, London W1V 5PA

© Marshall Cavendish Limited 1985

ISBN 0 600 50078 0

Typeset in Cheltenham by Elvins Ltd., Anlaby, England

Printed and bound by New Interlitho SpA., Italy

Introduction

Winemaking in the home has been practised for many years but it has become popular again recently as the price of commercial wines has risen more and more. *The Hamlyn Basic Guide to Winemaking* tells you everything you need to know about making palatable wines from the conventional grape or from natural ingredients like non-toxic fruit, vegetables or flowers, in fresh, canned or dried form. Wine for all occasions can be made and a taste for wine with different flavours can be acquired – an attractive wine can even be made from tree sap or tea!

The first section tells you all you need to know about wines and then you can find out how to get hold of all the different types of ingredients to make wine. All the necessary equipment is given and clear instructions for the winemaking methods are discussed in detail. You can start off making wine from kits and move on to making country wines. Remedies for potential problems like a wine turning acid or lacking character are given in chart-form. It is also suggested that you bottle some of your country wines in half-bottles so that you do not have to wait too long to taste them! The A-Z of recipes contains a choice of more than 50 different recipes for you to make and the last chapter on liqueurs can be experimented with when you have fully mastered the art of making wine.

All the text is clear and easy to follow and is accompanied by beautiful full colour pictures and specially commissioned black and white artworks. *The Hamlyn Basic Guide to Winemaking* will help you to make good-quality wines that will delight your friends and family and cost you a fraction of the price of wine you buy in the shops.

Contents

Chapter 1
All About Wines

Wines are one of the pleasures of life and before you start to make them you will need to know what wine actually consists of and the alcholic content that needs to be achieved. Broadly speaking, red, white or rosé wines can be made and these can then be divided into several different categories for drinking socially — table wines are the largest category and are normally drunk with meals. Wines can also be further distilled to make the stronger liqueurs or brandies or be fortified with a spirit to make a sherry or a port-type wine.

Winemaking probably started by accident when one of our ancestors stumbled on the enjoyable tastes and intoxicating effects of alcoholic fruit juices which had been fermented by the natural yeast present in the air.

Certainly wine was an everyday drink of the ancient Egyptians, Greeks, Cretans and during the Greek and Roman civilizations, wine was one of the main trade items – the other two were olive oil and grain. Wine was obviously produced by the Romans at home too, as there is record of a Roman cookbook written in the 1st century AD carefully recording a recipe for the perfect spiced wine with all the ingredients measured in scruples!

The Bible also contains many references to vineyards, grapes and wine pressing, including the famous story of Christ turning water into wine at a wedding celebration.

Nowadays, vineyards around the world are more extensive than they have ever been and wine is produced commercially in just about every country where vines will grow. Italy is one of the biggest wine producers, Germany, surprisingly, has a relatively small output. France, however, is the country that leads with wine production and has some of the world's best wines.

All About Wines

The taste of homemade wine will never be able to match up to the wonderful flavour of a quality commercial wine, but with experimentation and practice, a good-quality table wine, which will be praised by all your friends, can be made.

There has, in fact, been a great revival of home wine-making in the last 20 years especially as the price of commercial wines has increased so dramatically. Excellent wines can be made in the home from almost any non-toxic fruit, vegetable, grain and flower in the fresh, canned or dried form. Even tea or tree sap can be used to make an acceptable wine!

Making wines from organic ingredients can produce a variety of flavours, not always suited to everyone's palate, so if the taste of grape wine is preferred, grape juice concentrates can be purchased. These can make extremely good equivalents of commercial-type table wines. The concentrates are freely available from home winemakers' stores, DIY centres and large chemist chains. The specialist stores also stock all types of grain, dried and canned fruits and vegetables that are suitable for winemaking plus all the equipment and any additives that are necessary. The same equipment can be used time and time again and soon pays for itself. It is only the ingredients which need to be purchased or gathered for each new batch of wine.

Some of the world's classic wines always appear in the same shaped bottles and are normally drunk with a certain type of glass. From left to right: the French Burgundy, sparkling Champagne, Provence and Moselle bottle. Then appears the classic German rhine wine bottle, the Italian straw-covered flask for Chianti, the Portuguese rosé wine bottle and lastly the classic French Bordeaux bottle.

Wine content

Wines can be either dry, medium or sweet in flavour and they are a mixture of water, alcohol and various flavouring agents. They can be made from almost any natural product that can be fermented, but certain ingredients are necessary for flavour and the fermentation process. Wine is easily made from grapes because they contain all these ingredients. The grape juice normally contains a large proportion of sugar and the flavour is normally adequate without additives.

Yeasts are present in the grape skins so the juice will normally ferment naturally, but with other bases it may be necessary to add ingredients like acid, tannin, yeast and sugar. So to make wine the juices, known as the 'must', are extracted from the organic base being used and ingredients are added to compensate for any deficiencies in flavour. Yeast and sugar is then added and the fermentation vessel is kept at a certain temperature to encourage yeast action. Harmful bacterial must be kept out of the must and in a short while the liquid will start to froth and bubble indicating that the fermentation process has begun.

Fermentation

When the must starts to ferment the yeast enzymes feed on the sugar content and change it to ethyl alcohol and carbon dioxide gas. The yeast goes on feeding on the sugar until all the sugar has been used and the alcohol rises to such a level that the yeast is killed and fermentation stops. This normally occurs when the alcohol content reaches between 10–17% by volume. By this stage a deposit, known as 'lees', has formed at the bottom of the fermentation vessel. If any sugar is left, which has not been converted, the wine will have a very sweet flavour. Ideally, only the right amount of sugar should be added so that it is all fermented out to give the correct alcohol content and a dry wine. If a sweet wine is preferred, sweetening agents can be added after the fermentation process has ceased.

Alcohol content

The alcohol in wines is measured in '% alcohol by volume'. Most table wines have between 10–12% alcohol. Below the 10% alcohol level wine will probably not keep for more than three or four months. A white wine, low in alcohol, however, does make a very pleasant light drink during the hot summer months. Aperitifs, ports, sherries and dessert wines are usually stronger in volume – normally between 15–30% alcohol, but these have been fortified by the addition of brandy or a tasteless spirit like vodka. Liqueurs are normally distilled wines and are even stronger in volume and normally range between 30–75% in volume.

Wine classification

Wines can be red, white or pink (rosé). The actual colour of the wine will relate to the type of fruit or ingredient used to make it. When wine is made from grapes, however, it is the grape skins which determine the colour. Red grape wine can only be made from the skins of black grapes. If the skins were removed in the early stages of production, a white wine would result. Green grapes produce white wine. A rosé wine is really a combination wine, it is made from black grapes and the skins are left in the extracted juice for a short while only to leave a hint of colour, alternatively, red and white wines are mixed together.

Types of wine

Some wines could be loosely described as suitable for all occasions; they might be drunk mid-morning as an ideal pick-me-up, be used for cooking, drunk with lunch or dinner, or maybe even used as a basis for punches at parties. Tastes can vary enormously in wines so any exact classification should be viewed objectively, but there are recognized broad divisions which have evolved over the years as follows:

Aperitifs or appetizers. These are intended to stimulate the appetite before meals and to get the digestive juices flowing. They are normally wine-based and often quite dry and sharp in taste but with a delicate flavour. Sherries are in another category, but tend to be drunk as aperitifs.

Table wines are by far the largest category and the most widely available. They are generally drunk with meals and range from red to rosé to white, in many variations, and from sweet to dry. It has been found that the lighter, dryer, delicate white wines go extremely well with fish, veal, chicken or pork dishes, while the heavier, full-bodied red wines are more suited to red meats like beef, lamb and game. Rosé wines can be drunk with almost any meat and are particularly good when served well chilled with cold meats and pâtés. Sweet table wines are best with desserts. Most of the wines go well with cheese. Do not let tradition or custom deter you, however, if you are much happier drinking a white wine with beef, for example, then do so.

Dessert wines. These are rich wines with a strong flavour and tend to be rather sweet. They include sweet wines, ports, maderias and muscatels and can be ideal to drink with the pudding course or on their own after a meal. Port, particularly, is a very pleasant and popular wine to drink with a cheese course.

Champagne and sparkling wines. These are bubbling and effervescent wines served traditionally at weddings and celebrations. Sparkling wines can be made

successfully by home winemakers, but caution must be taken when making them as the extra fermentation in the bottle, which produces the bubbles, can cause a lot of pressure and result in nasty explosions.

Liqueurs and brandies. These tend to be drunk after meals, are alcohol based and are sometimes distilled from fruit or nuts or from wine. They are normally sweet to taste and are much stronger in alcohol volume than dessert wines. Some recipes are included in this book for liqueurs and fruit brandies using a base alcohol and fruit or other ingredients.

Fortifying wines

Fortification is when alcohol is added to a wine either to stop the fermentation process and leave some sugar unfermented, to give the wine better keeping qualities, or just to give the wine a higher alcohol content. Sherry, for example, is a fortified wine. To increase the alcohol level of a wine it has to be fortified with a spirit. For the home winemaker brandy or whisky can be used to fortify or a neutral-tasting spirit such as vodka or Polish white spirit can be used for making a port-type wine or a liqueur.

Country wine can be made to suit all occasions. From the left: Elderberry, a sweet, red dessert wine; Pea Pod Wine, a medium, white table wine; Blackberry, a sweet, red dessert wine; Gooseberry, a dry, white table wine and Orange, a dry, white aperitif.

11

Chapter 2
Making Your Wines

Many different ingredients can be used to make wine. You can make a grape-flavoured wine from concentrates or experiment with different flavours by making country wines from ingredients like fruit, vegetables, flowers, herbs — the possibilities are endless. All the equipment needed for winemaking is detailed in this chapter. The hydrometer, for example, is an essential item which helps you to achieve the right sugar level in a wine. The winemaking methods are illustrated with step-by-step colour pictures to really make them easy to understand. Potential problems can soon be resolved with the troubleshooting chart, and hints are given on the best ways to decant and serve your homemade wines.

Ingredients

If entirely new to winemaking, you are strongly recommended to try out one of the winemaker's kits now available. The kits contain a grape concentrate and everything you need, except sugar and water, to make 4.5 L (1 gal) or 23 L (5 gal) of wine. The wine produced needs to mature for about three months. Alternatively, an express kit will produce wine ready to drink in four to five weeks. The outlay for kits is not large and the instructions are simple and easy to follow.

Many different types of grape concentrates are available including named varieties like – hock, Burgundy, Bordeaux, Chablis, Chianti, claret, Sauternes, port, sherry and vermouth. Other fruit concentrates are available including apricot, bilberry, cherry, peach and elderberry. All the concentrates make 4.5 L (1 gal) of wine.

Fruits

Fruits tend to make better wines than other ingredients because they contain more acids and nitrogenous matter. Many early country wines were made simply by expressing the juice of a fruit or fruits and mixing that with a syrup or sugar boiled in water.

Traditionally, the quantity of fruit used per gallon of water was extremely high. Perhaps the fruit was of poorer quality than now, or perhaps palates then preferred a much stronger flavour; for whatever reason, wines were often extremely sweet and the use of less fruit would probably have produced a less tasty wine.

Today, although some reputable winemakers still use as much as, say, 2.7 kg (6 lb) of elderberries to make only 4.5 L (1 gal) of wine, on the whole much less fruit is used and lighter and drier wines are produced to be served as table wines rather than as the social and dessert wines produced in the past.

Methods of extracting the juice from the fruit have also changed. Until comparatively recently, it was usually extracted by steeping the fruit in water for up to three weeks at a time. Although the vessel would be covered with a cloth of some kind the floating fruit often developed a rich mould. Modern methods of juice extraction can prevent this problem, notably by the use of pectin-destroying enzymes protected by sulphite and shorter fermentation on the pulp.

Red juices from elderberries, blackberries, damsons and blackcurrants are best extracted by heating the crushed fruit to 85°C (176°F) for 15 minutes or so, then cooling or pressing. This method produces wines with better colour, higher alcohol and less bitterness than when the fruit is fermented on the pulp – the traditional method for making red wine in Europe. Called 'heat treatment', this method is superior to boiling the fruit which tends to produce a 'cooked' flavour in the wine, and can be

strongly recommended. Fruits that produce white wines can be treated in a similar way, although they should be heated to the lower temperature of 65°C (149°F). More often with white wine, however, the preference is to crush the fruit, add cold water, pectic enzyme and sulphite, cover and leave for twenty-four hours, and then ferment on the pulp for only three to four days. This method extracts the desired soluble ingredients without too many of the bitter flavours that can develop from long fermentation on the pulp.

Steam juice extractors, once popular, are now thought to produce a 'cooked' flavour and hazes in the wine, and are consequently losing some of their appeal. Blending fruit is gaining in popularity. Some winemakers strain out the solids after blending and discard them, using only the juice which they then dilute to make the must. Others argue that many valuable ingredients remain in the solids and are therefore wasted if the fruit is not fermented on the pulp at all. Many now ferment white fruit wines on the pulp for a few days, and then strain out the solids.

All fruit should be cleaned and washed before it is crushed. Always use the best quality available since stale or damaged fruit may already be infected with spoilage organisms. If windfall or damaged fruit must be used, cut away all bruised parts and maggot holes and sterilize the rest in a double strength sulphite solution. Frozen fruit makes successful wine provided that it is sulphited before freezing – otherwise it tends to oxidize as it thaws.

Stones must always be removed from fruits, although some pips or seed may be left in. Even more important, always avoid cracked fruit stones. If any are included, the glycosides present in the kernels may be converted into a poison called hydrogen cyanide. Avoid, too, the white pith of citrus fruit. It contains not only an unacceptably bitter flavour, but also pectin that causes haze in the wine.

Bananas are best used when the skins are black and the pulp brown. They are often used as an additive to wine and contribute body rather than flavour. One or two per 4.5 L (1 gal) are enough. Pineapples must be trimmed but need not be peeled. Soft fruits must be cleaned from their stalks and washed in cold water.

Canned fruits are available as pieces, pulps and purées, often in 1.8 kg (4 lb) cans, or larger. Varieties include apple, apricot, bilberry, blackberry, gooseberry, pineapple and rhubarb. These cans are extremely good value for people who want to make more wine than 4.5 L (1 gal). Dried fruits are also available from most winemakers' stores and include: dried apricots, bananas, bilberries, elderberries and flowers, peaches, raisins and sultanas. Buy seedless raisins or sultanas, if possible.

A wide selection of wild and cultivated fruits can be used to make satisfactory homemade wines.

14

Vegetables

The method of extracting the juice from vegetables remains the same as it has always been. The vegetables are cleaned, scrubbed, diced and boiled in water until they are tender. The cooking liquor (into which most of the nutrients from the vegetables will be transferred as the water boils) is then used for making the wine; the cooked vegetables can either be eaten or thrown away.

Fresh and tender vegetables straight from the garden can be trimmed, scrubbed and blended without cooking, and the juice and pulp fermented on the pulp for just a few days. Do not leave them too long or the resulting flavour will be overpowering rather than subtle. Since vegetables must be blanched before they are frozen there is no point in using frozen vegetables to make wine. Indeed, the best vegetable wines are made from really fresh vegetables, and any stale or poor-quality produce should be avoided. The results are simply not worth the effort.

Vegetables contain little in the way of acid or tannin and they should be added to make up the deficiency. The main contribution of vegetables to a wine is flavour.

Flowers

Flowers, unfortunately have even less to contribute to a wine than vegetables – nothing, in fact, but aroma and flavour. Everything else must be added, including body in the form of raisins or sultanas. Green leaves and stems should be avoided as they contribute a bitter flavour.

Flowers must be picked on a warm day when the blooms are fully open. Roses can be picked at petal fall but, where possible, other flowers should be picked as soon as they are fully open. Remove the petals or blooms from their stalks or calyx and place them in a large bowl. Pour on hot water and rub the petals gently with the back of a wooden spoon against the sides of the bowl. Cover and, when cool, add one Campden tablet and 5 ml (one tsp) of citric acid. Macerate the blooms against the sides of the bowl twice a day for three days then strain out and press the petals to remove the liquid. Use only the liquor to make the must.

Herbs

Parsley is one of the herbs most commonly made into wine, but many others can still be used. Gather the herbs when they are at their best: roots when the plant is dormant; leaves when just fully grown and before the flowers appear; flowers when just fully out. Leaves and flowers should be gathered as soon as the dew has evaporated and before the sun gets too hot. Handle them gently so as not to bruise them prematurely.

Herbs provide aroma and flavour only and everything else must be added to make wine. Prepare the essence from herb leaves and flowers in the same way as described for flowers. When the root is to be used, wash it clean, cut it up and boil until it is tender.

Spices

The most popular spice for making wine is ginger root. However, it can only be used as a flavouring ingredient. Freshly dried root, well bruised to open up the centre, is best. Cloves, coriander and caraway seeds may also be used to flavour wine.

Leaves

The most useful leaves are the summer prunings from vines and blackberry bushes; the young mature leaves of the blackcurrant bush; and the young mature leaves from the oak and walnut trees. Lime bracts are sometimes used, too, and of course tea leaves.

When the vine has produced fruit, excess foliage beyond the tiny bunch of grapes should be removed, leaving only one or two leaves to draw up the sap to feed the grapes rather than the extending shoots. Similarly, with blackberries – excessive side shoots must be kept in check. Cut the shoots with secateurs, wash them in clean running water, chop them up and pour boiling water over them. These prunings may be added to other musts to improve vinosity and flavour. Blackcurrant, oak and walnut leaves should be treated in the same way. Only a small number are needed and are best used as an additive to other wines. They freeze successfully and can be used at your convenience.

Flowers, cereals and vegetables, particularly, will need some extra natural additives added to make an acceptable country wine.

Saps

Several trees are suitable for tapping to obtain sap for making into wine: the birch, the sycamore, the walnut, the date palm, the coconut palm and the sugar maple. Several varieties of birch are particularly suitable – the silver birch, common in eastern and southern England; the white birch, common in western and northern England; and the dwarf birch, which grows in Scotland. Because of its high sugar content, the sap is used for making birch beer, a distinctive-flavoured soft drink, and therefore should also produce a good wine.

Early spring is the best time for tapping trees since the sap is flowing abundantly just prior to the opening of the leaf buds. *Never* tap a young tree since you may easily kill it. A mature tree suitable for tapping will have a diameter of from 20–22.5 cm (8–9 in).

Cereals

Cereals such as barley, maize, millet, rice and wheat, can be used to make wines of a sort. Millet wine, for instance, is widely produced in the country areas of China while in Japan the national drink, *sake*, is a wine made from rice. Flaked versions of cereals should be used whenever possible. Cereals provide gluten or body to a wine and some nitrogenous material and flavour, but it is advisable also to add some sultanas or raisins and, of course, acid and tannin. A special yeast, called *Saccharomyces diastaticus*, should be used with cereal musts since it ferments out some of the starch. The goodness is extracted from cereals by pouring boiling water on the cracked or flaked grains and stirring well.

Other Essential Ingredients

Yeast and nutrients

In early winemaking, fermentation was achieved by leaving a vessel of sweet grape juice in a warm place. The various yeast and other fungi and bacteria naturally present on the grape skins decomposed the sugar, turning it into alcohol and carbon dioxide. When fruit wines were made, fermentation was, again, often left to the wild yeasts present on the fruit, unless the liquor was boiled – then ale or bread yeast was spread on a slice of toast which was floated on the surface of the must. (The bread provided the yeast cells with nourishment in the form of nitrogen and vitamin B.) The great dangers in using these methods were, of course, that the juice or must would be inadequately yeasted and that there would be a consequent risk of infection from unwanted spoilage yeast and bacteria.

Only during the past thirty years have special wine yeasts become available for use at home. They are

Yeast and yeast nutrients are the two main ingredients which activate the process of fermentation in a wine.

marketed in several forms: as tablets; as putty-coloured granules; as liquids; and as a culture on an agar jelly slant in a sealed test tube. They are cultured in laboratories from pure yeast cells taken from grapes grown in areas that produce wines of distinctive styles, e.g. sherry, port, Burgundy, claret, Sauternes, and so on.

These special yeasts are vastly superior to bakers' and

ammonium sulphate, together with vitamin B are added. Grapes contain sufficient nutrient for the yeast and any recipes which contain a fair quota of grapes – whether fresh, dried as sultanas or raisins, or even liquid as concentrated grape juice – rarely need much, if any, additional nutrient. Granulated wine yeasts are often sold in sealed envelopes that also contain just enough nutrient to get the yeast cells off to a good start. Ingredients such as flowers, herbs and spices contain no nutrient and so 5 ml (1 tsp) of ammonium phosphate or sulphate crystals per 4.5 L (1 gal) should be added. The nutrient ensures a good fermentation and the conversion of the sugar to alcohol.

Clearly, a good wine yeast is an absolutely essential ingredient. To get the very best out of a good wine yeast it must be used in the proper way and under proper conditions – for instance, it ferments more efficiently if activated before it is added to the must, and also if all the wild yeasts and bacteria present in the must are killed or inhibited before it is added. To achieve a clean must purify it with sulphite.

Sulphite

The purifying qualities of sulphur have long been known to winemakers – sulphur candles used to be burned inside casks to kill off all spoilage organisms, originally called 'wild spirits'. Only in recent years has a compound of sulphur been developed that could be safely added to liquids to purify them. Two compounds are now in common use in winemaking: potassium metabisulphite and sodium metabisulphite. Both are available commercially in white crystalline powder form or compressed and sold as Campden tablets. One Campden tablet is sufficient to clean one 4.5 L (1 gal) of normal must, although two will be needed if the fruit is over-ripe or mouldy. Sulphite can, however, inhibit the activity of wine yeast and to avoid this possibility it is wise to add the sulphite to the must, then leave it for at least twenty-four hours before adding the yeast.

Acid

Another essential ingredient is acid. Yeast thrives best in an acid solution, and acid is also necessary to give freshness to a wine; without a sufficient supply the finished wine will taste medicinal and will not keep. Most fruits contain some acid: some, such as blackcurrants and lemons, contain a great deal; others, such as dates and figs, contain very little, if any. Flowers, vegetables, herbs, grains and spices contain no acid worth mentioning. When fruits are diluted with water or when ingredients without acid are used, some acid must be added to ensure a good fermentation and a good flavour.

The three most common acids are *citric*, found in all citrus fruit; *malic* found in apples, among many other

brewers' yeasts, and should be used in winemaking whenever possible. They are also preferable to the wild yeast and bacteria present on fruit. Apart from the beneficial yeast cells found on fruit, there are thousands of cells of spoilage fungi and bacteria mixed in with them and these pass into the wine. Often they cause 'off' flavours as well as preventing the wine yeast cells from fermenting adequately.

To supply the necessary nitrogen and vitamin B today, nutrient salts consisting of ammonium phosphate and fruits; and *tartaric* found only in grapes, which also contain some malic and citric acids. There is some controversy among expert winemakers as to which acid to add to a wine, since each one has its advantages and disadvantages. The great majority have settled for citric acid, but some do still prefer to use a blend of all three. In making such a decision, consideration should be given both to the quantity and type of acid already present in the fruit – and obviously more will be needed in flower and vegetable wines than in fruit ones. You can add acid either by adding acid fruit such as lemons to the wine or by adding acid crystals. When adding citric acid, bear in mind that the juice of one lemon is roughly equivalent to 5 ml (1 tsp) of crystals.

Tannin

Tannin gives red wine character and bite, and the addition of a little tannin can improve the flavour of all wines; it also helps the keeping qualities. All grapes contain tannin in their stalks, skins and pips, while some other fruits, such as pears, elderberries and blackberries, contain it only in their skin. Other plants are woefully short. Nowadays, it is usual to use grape tannin powder or liquid tannin at the rate of 2.5–5 ml per 4.5 L (½–1 tsp per 1 gal).

Pectin-destroying enzyme

Some fruits contain a lot of pectin, the substance which causes jams, marmalades and conserves to set. Pectin, however, can also cause a wine to appear hazy unless it is removed. We now know that pectin can be destroyed by enzymes that are usually present in fruits although not always in sufficient quantity to prevent a slight haze. It is sensible, then, to add a little pectin-destroying enzyme to those musts made from the fruits that are often used for jam-making: apricots, blackberries, blackcurrants, plums, raspberries and strawberries. When in doubt, 5 ml per 4.5 L (1 tsp per 1 gal) will always ensure the best possible juice extraction and a wine free from pectin haze.

Water

Ingredients such as flowers, herbs, grains and spices contain no water, and vegetables contain very little. Fruits contain varying quantities of water in the form of juice up to three-quarters of their weight, but these fruit juices are often highly acidic and need to be diluted with water. Clean water is essential, then, in the making of country wines. In most countries, a clean safe water supply is available in every home, but fresh spring water is excellent, too, and well water is safe so long as no poisonous matter can drain into it. Rainwater should always be filtered and boiled before use. It does not seem to matter significantly whether water is 'soft' or 'hard' although if there is a choice, preference should be given to

Adding pectin-destroying enzyme to some fruit wines helps to remove any haze. Sugar or sometimes honey is essential in winemaking to create the right alcohol level.

a medium or slightly hard water, because the many trace elements that it contains may help to create a slightly better bouquet and flavour. Distilled water produces dull, characterless wines.

Sugar

Apart from grapes grown in a warm atmosphere, no ingredient used for making wine contains enough natural sugar to ensure the creation of sufficient alcohol to make a good wine. Even grapes grown in Burgundy and through-out Germany sometimes do not develop sufficient natural sugar to make an adequate wine. Sugar is therefore added when necessary to help the process along.

Traditional recipes frequently called for the addition of 2 kg of sugar per 4.5 L (4 lb per 1 gal), but sugar in those days was less pure than it is today and contained a quantity of unfermentable matter; in addition, the common preference was for very much sweeter wines than is the norm today. An instrument called a saccharometer, which measured the approximate quantity of sugar in a must, was used more than 200 years ago. Today this same simple instrument is still used but is now called a hydrometer. This is used to control the quantity of additional sugar that must be added to produce a wine of approximately a given alcohol content.

The type of sugar added is of some importance. The least expensive and the most suitable is ordinary white granulated sugar. It is 99.95 per cent pure and there is no chemical difference between beet and cane varieties. Light brown and dark brown sugars can also be used but

20

immediately but ordinary sugar must first be split into the two by the enzyme called invertase which is secreted by the yeast cells. Ordinary sugar can be easily split into invert sugar: just boil 900 g (2 lb) of granulated sugar in 550 ml (1 pt) of water containing 5 ml (1 tsp) of citric acid crystals for about 20 minutes – when cool you have 1.2 L (2 pt) of invert sugar with a specific gravity of 1.300. Fructose and glucose powder are also available and can be used, although they are both more expensive than granulated sugar.

Finings

A variety of ingredients can be used to remove the haze that sometimes remains in a wine, even after the use of a pectin-destroying enzyme. Isinglass, marketed in the form of a gel, is today the most popular product. Bentonite, also marketed as a gel, is often used, so, too, is gelatine. These also remove some tannin which must be replaced. Directions for use are always given on the container.

they do impart both colour and flavour to wine and, clearly, are not to be recommended for white and golden wines unless, of course, you wish to create a tawny wine with a caramel overtone.

Before sugar, honey was used as a sweetener but it produced a mead rather than a wine for the honey taste dominated other flavours. A little white honey could be used effectively in flower wines but not more than 450 g per 4.5 L (1 lb per 1 gal). The quantity of granulated sugar should be reduced by 350 g (¾ lb) if honey is used.

There is no point in using cube, lump or loaf sugar since they are the same as granulated but more expensive because of their shaping process. Caster sugar dissolves very quickly, as does icing sugar, but both are more expensive in the shops than the granulated variety – although they are all chemically the same.

Milk sugar, called lactose, cannot be fermented by wine yeasts but is sometimes used to sweeten wines. It has only one-third of the sweetening power of granulated sugar, so you may have to use quite a lot of it to obtain the sweetness desired. Used at the rate of 75–100 g per 4.5 L (3–4 oz per 1 gal) it can improve a very dry wine.

Golden syrup may be used in much the same way as honey, with a similar rate of reduction in the amount of granulated sugar used. Like honey, about 25 per cent of the weight of syrup is water, so 450 g (1 lb) of honey or golden syrup is the equivalent of 350 g (¾ lb) of sugar.

Black treacle and molasses contain little fermentable sugar and possess an unacceptable flavour. Not more than 15 ml per 4.5 L (1 tsp per 1 gal) should be used for colouring or medicinal purposes if so required.

Invert sugar is simply ordinary granulated sugar that has been split into its two component sugars – fructose and glucose. Yeast cells can ferment fructose and glucose

Ingredients to avoid

As some fruits and flowers are poisonous, a basic rule to follow is not to make wines from any fruit that is not normally eaten fresh, canned or dried. Avoid known poisonous plants as the following list: acacia, aconite, alder, anemone, aquilegia, azalea, bane-berry, bella-donna, berberis, bitter almond, bay tree leaves, beech nuts, box tree leaves, black night-shade, bindweed, bluebell, bryony, dried broom flowers and seeds, buckthorn, buddleia, buttercup, campion, celandine, charlock, cineraria, clematis, clover, contoneaster, columbine, cow-bane, crocus, crowfoot, chrysanthemum, cuckoo-pint, cyclamen, daffodil, dhalia, deadly nightshade, delphinium, dwarf elder, fool's parsley, figwort, foxglove, fungi of all kinds, geranium, gladiolus, goosefoot, green potatoes, all members of the helebore family, hemlock, herbane, holly, honeysuckle (both flowers and berries), horse chestnut flowers and conkers, hydrangea, hyacinth, iris, ivy, jasmine, jonquil, laburnum, laurel, lilac, lilies of the valley, lilies of all kinds, lobelia, lucerne, lupins, marsh marigolds, meadow rue, mezereon, mistletoe, monkshood, narcissus, orchids, pheasant's eye, peony, poppy, privet, ragwort, rhododendron, rhubarb leaves, snowdrop, spearwort, spindleberries, spurge, sweet pea, thorn apple, tobacco plant, tomato stems and leaves, traveller's joy, tulip, wood anemone, woody nightshade, yew.

Also beware of picking flowers, leaves or plants that could have been sprayed with weedkiller as these too could be dangerous.

Equipment

Certain items of equipment are needed for winemaking. In actual fact, the expense involved in acquiring the basic essentials is surprisingly modest and most investment in additional equipment can be left until such time as you feel sufficiently enthusiastic about your hobby to indulge in the extra expense. Many common items of household kitchen equipment can also be used, reducing even further the basic outlay necessary before you can start to make your own wine.

If you plan to make wine just with concentrates initially, you will not need the mashing equipment detailed. If you have bought a full kit you will find all the necessary equipment items have been included.

Before you start your winemaking you will need to follow some general rules:

1. Always avoid the following: lead-glazed earthenware jars; lead piping; zinc baths, buckets or boilers; chipped enamel pails, funnels, saucepans or containers; brass or copper pans or other utensils. Acids in wine react with the exposed metals mentioned above to form poisonous salts.
2. Never use metal utensils unless they are made of silver or the best quality stainless steel. High grade aluminium pans may be used briefly for boiling low acid ingredients, but the contents of the pan should never be allowed to stand in the vessel for any length of time.
3. Coloured polythene equipment is also suspect. Cadmium, which is poisonous, is sometimes used for colouring, and the plasticizer can react with the acid or alcohol. It is always safer to use the natural plastic, polypropylene or polycarbonate utensils sold in home brew shops or department stores.

Essential items

Mashing bin

The first item you will need is a vessel in which to mash fruit (or vegetables if you use the pulping method for very fresh produce) and prepare the must for conversion into wine. In the past glazed earthenware crocks and oak tubs, cut in half, were used, but when polythene first became available in the 1950s, small trash bins with lids of this material became popular. Nowadays, however, purpose-made polythene bins have largely taken their place. These bins are colourless, inert to acids and are light and easy to clean. They come supplied with close-fitting lids. They are sufficiently translucent for you to be able to see the level of the liquid inside and most of them are graduated both in metric and imperial measurements of volume.

Standard sizes can contain 12, 15 or 25 litres of liquid, sufficient to make 2, 3 or 5 gallons of wine, respectively. It is unwise to fill them too full, even although each bin is fitted with a strong carrying handle, for they are flexible and the contents could spill when carried. The number of bins required depends on the quantity of wine you intend to make at any one time, but certainly several, of different sizes, would be useful. They are easy to store, too, especially if you buy graded sizes, for they can stack inside one another when not in use.

Masher

You will also need something to crush the fruit or vegetables. A potato masher is excellent for soft fruits, provided that it is made from nylon, stainless steel or heavily coated chrome. Other metals should be avoided.

A block of oak or other heavy non-resinous wood on the end of a broom handle does well for crushing harder fruits and vegetables. Purpose-made mangle-like fruit crushers can be bought if larger quantities have to be handled regularly, but they are too bulky and expensive if you propose to make only a few gallons of wine at a time. Electric blenders are becoming increasingly popular 'mashers', and steam juice extractors can also be used. Mincing and meat grinding machines may be used subject to the proviso that has been mentioned about metal.

A recent innovation is a stainless steel blade on a shaft of the same metal that can be fitted to an electric drill. To use it, fit the lid of a bin between the blade and the drill and fill the bin with washed and perfect fruit. Now fit the lid to the bin, switch on, move the spinning blade up and down a few times and the fruit will be completely pulped.

Fermentation vessel

Fermentation can be carried out in a mashing bin – indeed, this is essential when fermenting on the pulp. Some mashing bin lids are fitted with a grommet that can be removed so that an airlock can be fitted. This is especially useful when fermenting more than 4.5 L (1 gal) of must. Other bins are fitted with draw-off taps.

The vast majority of winemakers today, however, use colourless glass demijohns called jars or jugs for fermenting their wines. In the UK they are currently available in 2.3 and 4.5 L sizes (½ and 1 gal), but many hold slightly more – some up to as much as 5 litres. They are, nevertheless, widely referred to as 'gallon jars'. They are ideal for the purpose because they are inert to acids; can be easily washed and sterilized; activity in them can be seen; the narrow neck takes a bored bung and airlock that seals the jar effectively; and most have small carrying handles fitted to the neck.

Their disadvantage is that they are brittle and are, therefore, breakable if not handled with care. They have also become quite expensive. They are so convenient, however, that they are frequently used for storage as well as fermentation. Since it may be necessary, with some wines, to store them for a year before bottling, possession of several jars at least is essential for the active winemaker.

A wide range of inexpensive equipment is readily available for the home winemaker.

Some larger glass carboys in a protective cover are also available in 25 and 55 L sizes (which make 5½ and 12¼ gal of must).

An unbreakable transport polycarbonate container has now been developed but is still at present rather expensive for popular use. A laminated polythene bag containing a nylon 66 or Sarinex centre layer that makes it vapour-proof has also recently been marketed. It is fitted with a rigid neck to accommodate a bored bung and airlock, and a tap-like cover, and is supported in a vinyl-coated cardboard carton. It is unbreakable, easy to clean and sterilize, and can be used for fermentation, storage and serving. It can also be folded away when not in use.

Storage vessels

Glass fermentation vessels can also be used for storage. If you have a limited supply of demijohns but have glazed earthenware jars, these can be used instead. Although they are heavy to handle and vulnerable if used carelessly, they do have the advantatge of insulating the wine from sudden changes in temperature, and they keep it cool and dark. Oak casks may, of course, also be used and these are specially recommended to mature red wines in quantities of 25 L (5½ gal) and more. Smaller casks are not suitable because the ratio of surface to volume causes excessive oxidation of the wine.

Polythene containers are not suitable since they are not vapour-proof. Plastic casks of the type used for draught beer can sometimes be used for the temporary storage of wine but there is still some slight uncertainty about the solubility of plastic in the presence of alcohol over a long period of time.

Airlocks

Airlocks, or water seals as they are sometimes called, are used to exclude air from the must during fermentation while permitting gas to escape. There are several types that come in many different shapes and sizes but all work on the same principle. There are two main types. One is U-shaped with a spherical bulb on each wing of the 'U', and usually made of glass, the other consists of a small cylinder into which is fitted a narrower cylinder, and is usually made of plastic. Both end in a short tube which fits into a bored bung. A little water or sulphite solution is poured into the container thus forming a lock. It is then fitted into the hole in the bung, which is pushed into the neck of the fermentation jar in order to form an airtight seal. The gas given off during fermentation will build up sufficient pressure to force its way through the water or sulphite solution and escape into the outside air with a quiet 'plop'. Because of this the progress of fermentation can be easily monitored.

Siphon

A siphon, in its simplest form, is a long length of rubber or plastic tubing which is used at the end of the fermentation period to suck off the new wine from its sediment. More sophisticated versions can be fitted with a glass J-tube at one and and a small tap at the other, or with a blocked end above which four holes have been drilled. To use the siphon, one end of the tube is inserted into the wine which must then be sucked into the tube until it is full. The outer end is temporarily closed and placed into a sterilized container for storage situated at a lower level than the wine vessel. The tube is then opened and the wine will flow steadily into the lower vessel. This should be done carefully since it is imperative not to disturb the sediment. The J-tube siphon sucks the wine down from the top and the blocked end type sucks it in from the sides; both are ideal as they leave the sediment undisturbed.

23

Hydrometer

Almost the only scientific, although simple, instrument required in amateur winemaking is the hydrometer (sometimes called a saccharometer) which, in appearance, resembles a thermometer. The stem contains a graduation of figures which indicate the gravity or weight of the volume of liquid being measured compared with the same volume of water. In home winemaking and brewing the additional weight is almost entirely sugar so the instrument for all practical purposes measures the quantity of sugar dissolved in a must, and thus enables you to calculate how much additional sugar to add to produce a wine of a given alcoholic content. It is used in conjunction with a slim jar slightly taller than the hydrometer, which is called a 'trial jar'. Some liquid to be tested is poured into the trial jar and the hydrometer inserted into it to measure the quantity of sugar present.

Bottles

You will need wine bottles, preferably of coloured glass to exclude the light, in which to age your wine. Use empty commercial wine bottles, after first soaking off old labels. Wash, drain, dry and store them upside down in a bottle carton until required. A bottle brush would be useful to clean congealed sediment from the sides and the bottle punt. Larger brushes might be required to clean demijohns, particularly under the shoulder which often becomes marked from matter thrown up during the fermentation process.

The hydrometer and fermentation vessel are winemaking items which are always in constant use. When the wine is bottled, attractive labels and foil capsules can be used to give your wine a professional touch.

Equipment

Corks and labels

Cylindrical corks and a corking tool to insert them in the bottle are essential. The corking tool can be a simple flogger, a shaped cylinder in which the softened cork is placed and then hammered via a wooden piston into the bottle, or a hand machine in which the cork is levered into the bottle. Decorative labels and coloured foil or plastic capsules complete the very professional appearance of the bottle.

Wine racks

You will need somewhere to store the finished bottle of wine, and a wine rack is both a desirable acquisition and a sensible one for the purpose. Traditional wooden and metal racks can be purchased to fit any storage space and any number of bottles. Other metal, wooden or plastic bottle crates can be used, of course, including strong cardboard bottle cartons. But these do vary in quality and strength and only the strongest are safe when stored on their sides.

Filters

Sometimes a wine will not clear completely on its own and needs to be fined or filtered. A selection of different brands of filters are available, one particular model incorporating a force pump filters the wine in a few minutes. There are also several fining and filtering materials that clear wine of all cloudiness or haze.

Record cards

You should complete a record card for each wine you make, giving details of ingredients, quantities, methods, dates and results. The cards can be purchased ready printed or devised from a luggage label.

Smaller items

Many homes will already have a number of the smaller pieces of equipment useful to a winemaker – items such as wooden spoons, measuring jugs, a pair of kitchen scales, a polythene funnel or two, a nylon strainer, perhaps a kitchen thermometer and a preserving or large boiling pan. Such items need not be exclusively reserved for winemaking, although care should be taken to wash and sterilize them before use. It is best to avoid using utensils or equipment used in the making of pickles and chutneys.

Extra items

Heaters

Fermentation needs to be conducted in a warm place, the ideal temperature is 21°C (70°F). In very cold places it may be necessary to stand the jar on a thermal pad or surround it with a thermal belt to provide the necessary warmth. Suitable immersion heaters are also available and their advantage is that they can be attached to a thermostat to maintain the right temperature throughout the fermentation. Some winemakers adapt cupboards with insulation and electric 'black-heat' cylinders. In very warm weather it may, conversely, be necessary to provide some means of cooling the jars of must with fans or cold water.

Fruit press

This is an item which is only necessary if you intend to make a great deal of fruit wine. It is basically a wooden box with an open top and slotted sides through which the extracted juice flows into its base. Special pulp bags are usually available with a fruit press. To use the press, wash it with a sulphite solution, then place the bag of pulp in the press. Pressure should be erratic rather than steady. As the flow begins to slow down, increase the pressure then leave it until the flow slows again, then increase the pressure again and so on. After a while, release the pressure entirely, remove the bag, stir up the pulp, replace the bag in the press and resume the pressure. Continue these processes until the pulp becomes a dry 'cake'.

Hygiene

All equipment must be kept scrupulously clean, and sterilized before use. A chlorine-based sterilizer is excellent for removing stains and cleaning dirty jars and bottles as well as plastic vessels. Equipment sterilized in this way should be thoroughly rinsed in cold water to remove the chlorine. Chlorine-based sterilizers should neve be used to sterilize ingredients, only equipment.

Sodium metabisulphite, especially when reinforced with citric acid, makes an effective sterilizing agent, especially for equipment that is otherwise clean. It is also safe and strongly recommended for sterilizing ingredients, especially fruit. This agent has the additional advantage of being an anti-oxidant, in other words it prevents oxidation or browning and the consequent deterioration in colour, bouquet and flavour.

Sodium metabisulphite is available as a powder and in tablet form, sold under the name Campden. One Campden tablet contains 0.44 g of sodium metabisulphite and releases 50 parts per million of the sterilizing bacteria and fungicide, sulphur dioxide, when dissolved in 4.5 L (1 gal) of water, must or wine. This is a normal and adequate dose but may safely be doubled or trebled when necessary.

Some winemakers dissolve the powder and some citric acid in water and keep this solution well sealed in a suitable bottle stored in a cool place. In these circumstances it will retain its sterilizing properties for several months.

To make up a typical solution, dissolve 100 g of sodium metabisulphite and 10 g of citric acid in 1 L of cold water (2 oz of sodium metabisulphite and 1 tsp citric acid in 1 pt of cold water). Five milligrams (1 tsp) of either of the above solutions is equal to one Campden tablet.

One Campden tablet or 5 ml (1 tsp) of the solution dissolved in 550 ml (1 pt) of cold water makes a powerful sterilizing solution for finally rinsing jars, bottles, corks and all other equipment before use. One tablet or 5 ml (1 tsp) in 2.25 L (½ gal) of water is adequate for washing fruit before use. One Campden tablet or 5 ml (1 tsp) added to 4.5 L (1 gal) of wine after racking prevents infection and oxidation. The wise use of sulphite prevents countless ailments and ensures sound wine.

Sodium metabisulphite and potassium metabisulphite are quite cheap. Campden tablets are a little more expensive but no winemaker should ever be without an adequate stock.

Before you start winemaking, always ensure that you sterilize all your equipment thoroughly before use.

Hygiene in winemaking has advanced considerably since the early days of sterilization. Campden tablets have been known for a long time for thier preservative qualities but is only since the 1960s that their efficiency at sterilizing both equipment and ingredients has been widely known. Nowadays, every sensible winemaker rinses and sterilizes all equipment before use with a solution of sodium metabisulphite and citric acid to prevent tainting a wine. The regular use of Campden tablets in sterilizing wines is so accepted that specific quantities are not mentioned in the detailed recipes – it is presumed that the winemaker will keep adequate stocks.

The purity of yeast now available and the habit of adding a cultured wine yeast to a sterilized must has helped improve the quality of country wines considerably. The use of modern equipment – polythene bins, fermentation vessels and air locks have helped to keep out spoilage organisms in the air and improve the quality of wine produced. Hydrometers, too help to accurately control the amount of sugar used and the alcohol strength achieved in a wine. All the recipes included detail a certain amount of sugar, related to the wine and ingredients used. This can only be approximate, however, depending on the sweetness of the ingredients, but with the aid of the hydrometer you can add more sugar for a sweeter wine or ferment the must longer for a dryer, stronger wine.

Making wine from kits

Before you start making wine from organic ingredients, you might well want to start with basic winemaking using grape or fruit concentrates. These are very easy to use but the basic method for making a dry red wine is included, accompanied by detailed step-by-step pictures so that you can clearly understand how the winemaking process works.

Method
Pour the grape concentrate into a 4.5 L (1 gal) fermentation jar and add 3.4 L (6 pt) of warm water 38°C (100°F). Stir in 225 g (½ lb) of sugar and continue stirring until it has dissolved. Allow to cool to room temperature – about 21°C (70°F).

It is possible to add the sugar in two separate stages but there is more possibility of the fermentation stopping and a greater risk, of infection to the wine if this is done.

When the temperature is 21°C (70°F) add the yeast prepared in a starter bottle, the citric acid and the yeast nutrient, if required.

Partially fill the airlock with sterilized water and place it in the bored bung, making sure that the two bubble shapes are level. Fit the bung carefully into the top of the jar. Leave the jar in a warm place for 7–10 days. Check

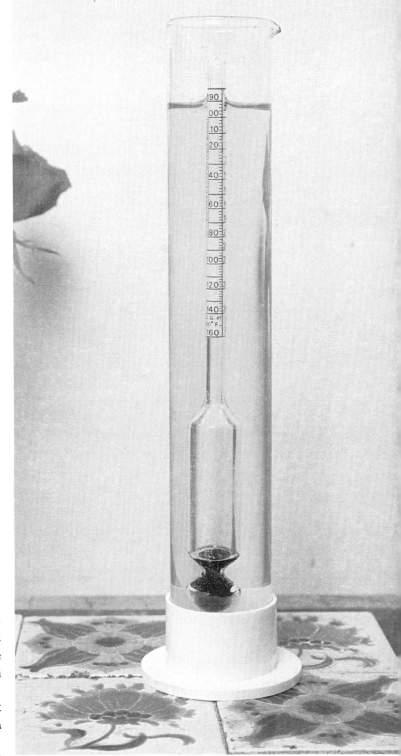

The hydrometer is essential in winemaking to measure the sugar level of a fermenting wine.

that the airlock is bubbling constantly and evenly.

After 7–10 days the fermentation jar should be topped up with cold water.

1 Pour the grape concentrate into a 4.5 L (1 gal) fermentation jar and add 3.4 L (6 pt) warm water 38°C (100°F).

2 Stir in 225 g (½ lb) sugar and continue stirring until it has dissolved. Allow to cool to room temperature about 21°C (70°F).

3 Add the yeast, citric acid and yeast nutrient, if required (see your kit's instructions to see which ingredients to add).

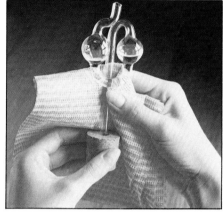

4 Partially fill the airlock with sterilized water and fit into the bung. Make sure that the two bubble shapes are level.

5 Fit the bung carefully into the top of the jar and leave the jar in a warm place for about 7–10 days. Then top up with cold water.

6 Leave the wine to ferment for 4–5 weeks in a warm place where the temperature is constant, such as an airing cupboard.

Fermentation

The best temperature for fermentation is between 21°–25.5°C (70°–78°F). During the summer months this is no problem as long as you put the fermentation vessel in a warm place where the temperature is constant. However, during the winter you may find the temperature is dropping below the right level or that it is fluctuating due to thermostatically controlled heating systems. If this is the case, you can either keep the fermentation jar in an airing cupboard, if you have one, or you can use one of the heaters which are available.

The wine must be left alone for four or five weeks until all the bubbles cease. When you think the fermentation has finished, you can draw off a sample with a siphon and test the specific gravity to see whether you have a dry,

medium or sweet wine. When the hydrometer reading is between .990 and 1.000 the wine can be siphoned into the second container. Add 225 g (½ lb) of sugar and two more Campden tablets now if a sweeter wine is wanted.

Racking

To siphon off the wine, put the full jar at a higher level than the empty one. Put either the blocked end of your pump or the glass U-bend of the ploythene tubing into the full jar. To start the flow, either pump the pump or suck the tube. When the flow has started, place the end of the siphon into the empty vessel until it is full. If you are filling more than one container just transfer the siphon from vessel to vessel until the siphoning is completed. Add one Campden tablet which will stabilize the wine during

7 Draw off a sample of the wine and test the specific gravity with the hydrometer, which should read between .990 and 1.015.

8 Siphon the wine into the second jar by putting the blocked end of a pump or the U-bend end of polythene tubing into the full jar.

9 Add a Campden tablet to the container and finings, if using. Leave to clear – up to 4 weeks without finings or 2 weeks with.

10 For sweet wine, add another 225 g (½ lb) sugar, 2 more Campden tablets and leave for at least another 12 weeks.

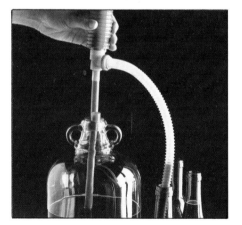

11 Siphon the wine into your bottles, filling up to 12 mm (½") away from where the bottom of the cork will be when it is in place.

12 Cork with straight wine bottle corks, using a corking machine, or polythene stoppers. Leave for at least 3–4 weeks before drinking.

storage until it is ready for bottling. If you are using a filter or finings, use them at this stage.

Leave the wine to completely clear, which can take up to four weeks.

Bottling and corking
If using wine corks, soak them in warm water containing 15 ml (1 tbsn) of sterilizing solution prior to bottling. If using polythene stoppers, sterilize them with the rest of the equipment.

Siphon the wine into your bottles filling to 12 mm (½ in) from the bottom of where the cork will be. Cork the bottles with a corking machine or insert the polythene stoppers by hand. Leave the wine for at least 3–4 weeks before drinking. The wine will be better still if left longer than

this. Label and date the bottles so that you will know what the wine is and when it is ready to drink. Plastic or foil capsules can also be added to the necks of the bottles. Always store the wine horizontally to ensure that the corks are moist.

Making express wine
Wine made with this sort of kit is made in the same way as other wines but is produced more quickly. The fermentation takes only about 7–10 days. It then takes a week or two to clear in the second container. Then it is bottled and left for about another week. With this sort of kit you can be drinking the wine after about three to six weeks. But it may take a little longer than this and also the wine will improve if it is left longer in the bottles.

Making country wines

Once you have mastered making wine from concentrates you will be keen to progress to more involved winemaking using natural ingredients.

First, the various primary ingredients must be assembled and prepared: select your fruit, vegetables, flowers, herbs, leaves, saps, cereal or spice, clean as necessary and place them in a bin for pulp fermentation or into a jar if it is all liquid. If you are making a fruit wine, add pectic enzyme and one Campden tablet per 4.5 L (1 gal) at this point to dissolve the pectin. Leave for twenty-four hours.

Using your hydrometer

Next day, take your first hydrometer reading to discover the sugar content of the must. Strain a quantity of the must into a trial jar and place the hydrometer in the jar. Wait until it stops bobbing and twisting. When it is quite still it will float and the surface of the must will indicate a reading on the chart of the stem. (In an apple must, for example, the reading might be 1.032, in a grape must it might be as high as 1.076. A flower or herb must without sultanas or seedless raisins or sugar could read only 1.002 and a vegetable must 1.006.)

Refer to the table on page 102. Find your hydrometer reading in the left-hand column. Level with it in column 3 you will find the weight of the sugar already present in your gallon of must. Make a note of this figure. Now look at the potential alcohol table in the right-hand column and select the approximate amount of alcohol you would like in your finished wine.

Looking again at column 3, you will find level with the alcohol percentage, the *total* amount of sugar that you will need in your must. From this deduct the amount of sugar already present. The difference is the amount of sugar to add. If sultanas or raisins are to be included in the recipe, you will need to allow for their natural sugar content. A large amount of their weight consists of fermentable sugars.

An example: The hydrometer reading of your fruit must is 1.020. This is equal to 275 g (9 oz) of sugar in 4.5 L (1 gal). You are planning to add 225 g (½ lb) of sultanas or raisins, the equivalent of 150 g (5 oz) of sugar in 4.5 L (1 gal). So already accounted for is the equivalent of 400 g (14 oz) of sugar. You would like an alcohol content of 12% in the finished wine and the table indicates that a total of 1100 g (2 lb 6½ oz) of sugar will be needed. Deduct the 400 g (14 oz) already accounted for, and you will see that 700 g (1 lb 8½ oz) of sugar still needs to be added. Of course, merely by adding sugar, you will increase the volume of the must. To allow for that increase, you will need to add one-eighth more sugar than indicated in the table, in this case, about another 90 g (3 oz). So the total amount of additional sugar will be 800 g (1 lb 11 oz).

But many country wines, especially those made from a

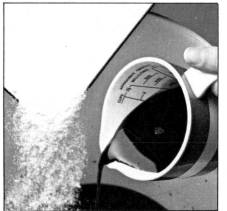

1 To make a country wine, remove the fruit from stalks and put in a fermentation bin. Pour over 2.3 L (4 pt) boiling water.

2 When cool, add 1 Campden tablet dissolved in a little of the liquid and 1.1 L (2 pt) water. Stir and leave 24 hours with the lid on.

3 Add the sugar, citric acid, pectic enzyme, wine yeast and yeast nutrient and leave to ferment on the pulp for 7 days.

4 Strain must through straining bag into a 4.5 L (1 gal) jar. Add cold water to make up wine to shoulder of jar.

vegetable, cereal or herb base are often stronger than 12%. Moreover, some winemakers prefer to drink their wines not with meals but on social occasions. A larger quantity of sugar is therefore necessary, not only to increase the alcohol content slightly but also to sweeten the wine to some extent.

The recipes in this book have taken into account not only the average sugar content of the base ingredient and the sugar content of the sultanas or raisins, but also the probable alcohol content and the increased volume of must in recommending the approximate amount of sugar to add. Nevertheless, hydrometer readings should still be taken to adjust the added sugar accordingly.

Acid and tannin

The acid and tannin content of the wine need to be considered now. Many recipes recommend the inclusion of acid in the form of lemon and/or orange juice because this was the traditional form of adding acid. The zest in citrus fruit skin can also add emphasis to the flavour of the base ingredient. But these fruits may be replaced with citric acid crystals if this is more convenient. Generally, a non-acid base needs 10 ml (2 tsp) for a light dry wine and 15–20 ml (3–4 tsp) for a sweeter, stronger wine. Fruit wines need less, depending on the acidity of the fruit. For example, blackcurrants need no extra acid at all, while dates and figs contain no acid and need a full quantity.

Tannin improves the character and longevity of a wine, especially fruit wines. Black grapes, elderberries, blackberries and pears usually contain sufficient tannin in their skins, but other fruits, especially those used to make a red wine, need the addition of up to 5 ml (1 tsp) of tannin powder of half a cup of cold tea.

The basic must is now prepared with the right amount of sugar, acid and tannin; the next stage is to add the yeast so that fermentation may begin.

Fermentation

It is important to use a pure wine yeast, preferably already activated, to ferment wine. Follow the instructions supplied with the tablet, sachet or phial of yeast to activate it. Alternatively, you can dissolve the juice of half an orange with 5 ml (1 tsp) of sugar and the wine yeast in a cupful of cold boiled water. Leave the mixture loosely covered in a warm place for a few hours – you will soon see signs of activity.

Yeast cells also need some nourishment in the form of nitrogen, which they can obtain from most fruits and vegetables or from ammonium salts. A small quantity of nutrient salts is usually enclosed in the sachet with the yeast, but if you are using a liquid or tablet yeast then add 2.5 ml (½ tsp) of nutrient salts to the must – especially when the base is flowers, leaves or herbs, even if raisins or sultanas are also being used.

Yeast ferments best between 15°C (59°F) and 24°C (75°F), but will tolerate both lower and higher

5 Fit the bung, leave for 7–10 days then top up with cold water. Leave to ferment for 3–5 weeks in a warm place.

6 Draw off sample of wine and test specific gravity which should read between .990 and 1.015. Siphon wine into second jar.

7 Add a Campden tablet and finings, if using, and leave to completely clear. This can take up to 3 months.

8 Siphon the wine into bottles and cork them. Leave at least 6 months before you start to drink the wine.

temperatures. It prefers a steady, even, unfluctuating temperature but, again, is tolerant of minor fluctuations. Experience shows that white wines develop best when fermented at around 16°C (61°F) and red wines when fermented at around 20°C (68°F).

Fermenting on the pulp. Fermentation on the pulp is usually in a polythene bin with some headroom. Keep the bin loosely covered with a clean towel or similar thick cloth, or with a sheet of polythene tied down with wool, string or thin elastic, so that the dust and microbes can be kept out yet the fermentation gas can escape. The pulp should be kept submerged with a sterilized dinner plate or with something similar – but with nothing metallic. If this is not possible, press the pulp down into the must twice each day. There is also always the danger that the pulp might become the breeding ground for spoilage organisms, especially *Mycoderma aceti*, the vinegar bacillus.

Fermentation on the pulp should not extend beyond a few days since unwanted substances tend to get extracted by the increasing quantity of alcohol as it is being formed.

Straining. After the first fermentation on the pulp, strain out the pulp through a nylon strainer or bag and drain dry. If the material is still fairly hard it should be pressed to extract as much juice as possible. You can use your hands or a small fruit press for this. When the pulp is dry, remove it from the bag.

Fermenting out. Stir the relevant amount of sugar into the strained must. Sometimes frothing will occur; always stir the sugar until it has dissolved. When the frothing has subsided, pour the must into a fementation jar. Fit an airlock into the jar. First, however, soften the bored bung in warm water and then screw the stem of the airlock into the hole in the bung until it fits tightly. In the same way, screw the bung into the neck of the jar until it will go no further. Finally, pour in a little sulphite solution to form the lock, tie on a completed record card or label and leave the jar in a warm position.

If you are using a standard demijohn and are making 4.5 L (1 gal) of wine, then the water, sugar and possibly juice from the base ingredient will produce more than enough must to fill the jar. Pour the excess into a sterilized bottle placed alongside the jar. The neck of the bottle should be plugged with cotton wool to keep out dust and micro-organisms, yet still allow the carbon dioxide to escape.

Normally fermentation takes about three weeks. Sometimes, however, with a strong yeast, the right temperature and the perfect balance of acid and nutrient, fermentation will finish in a week. On other occasions it may take six weeks or even longer, especially in low temperatures. There is nothing wrong, and long, slow fermentations are thought to produce the best flavoured wines. On rare occasions, fermentation will stop before it is expected to do so. First check with the hydrometer that the specific gravity of the must remains high. If fermentation has finished because all the sugar has been converted into alcohol and carbon dioxide, the hydrometer will sink in the new wine until the reading shows between 0.990 and 1.000. If this is so, the next stage of maturation can begin.

A 'stuck' fermentation. If the reading is still quite high, however, say 1.042, then fermentation has become 'stuck' for some reason. It may be that the must has become too hot or too cold and the yeast is, therefore, not working. Move the jar to a different place where the temperature is appropriate and steady. Meanwhile, check over the record card and make sure that you have included sufficient acid and nutrient as recommended in the recipe, for a lack of either could cause fermentation to stick. If in any doubt, remedy the situation at once, by adding the quantity of acid recommended in the recipe and about 2.5 ml (½ tsp) of yeast nutrient.

If fermentation does not soon start as a result of your actions, pour the contents of the jar into another jar, splashing the must into the receiving jar so that a quantity of oxygen is absorbed and the yeast stimulated to enlarge its colony.

The record card may also indicate that so much sugar was added that the yeast has reached the limit of its alcohol tolerance and cannot convert the remaining sugar. Most yeast can ferment up to about 14% alcohol, although a few can do better than this if the conditions are just right. If this is the cause of the fermentation stopping, then you will either have to drink the oversweet wine or blend it with one that is too dry.

If too much sugar is not the cause and fermentation still fails to resume, then the cause is probably due to the dying off of a weak yeast colony. Activate a fresh yeast in a starter bottle and, when it is fermenting well, add an equal quantity of stuck must to the starter and transfer it to a larger bottle. When this quantity is fermenting well add another equal volume of the stuck must and again transfer the fermentation to a still larger container. Repeat this process until all the stuck must has been added to the fermentation. Adding a fresh yeast to a stuck must rarely starts a fermentation. You must add it to the fermenting yeast in small doses and then only when the last dose is fermenting well.

Prolonged fermentation. A very strong wine can be made in a somewhat similar manner. Begin the fermentation in the usual way and slowly add more and more sugar over a period of time so that the tolerance of the yeast can be gradually built up. Tokay and Madeira yeasts are the most tolerant, followed by sherry and port. When adding the sugar, remove some of the must, stir in the sugar and, when it is dissolved, return the sweetened

Making a good-quality fruit wine can be a straightforward procedure providing every step is carefully monitored.

must to the jar and the excess to the bottle. Pour the must slowly so as not to cause foaming. Stand the jar and bottle on a tray or in a polythene bag in case there is any overflow during the fermentation.

Use the hydrometer frequently during a prolonged fermentation to ensure that the sugar is not added too soon. Wait until the specific gravity has fallen, say, to 1.006, and then add enough sugar to raise it, say, ten units to 1.016. When the gravity again falls to 1.006 repeat the process and so on. In this way one can produce a wine with the maximum amount of alcohol – up to 18% and then sweeten it to taste. It is always preferable to add sugar to suit your taste rather than to have to drink a wine that is too sweet.

Such a prolonged fermentation needs plenty of acid and nutrient as well as an even temperature around 20°C (68°F). The addition of 5 ml (1 tsp) of citric acid and half that quantity of nutrient is therefore a wise precaution.

Stopping the fermentation. Sometimes a sweet, low-alcohol wine of, say, 12% is wanted. This can be achieved in two ways: by sweetening a dry wine of 12% with lactose or saccharin or, alternatively, fermentation can be terminated when the wine still contains some sugar. To do this, move the jar to a cool place for a few days to slow down the fermentation and encourage the settling of the sediment, then siphon the clearing wine into another jar containing a 1 g tablet of potassium sorbate and a Campden tablet. The fermentation process will stop almost immediately and the wine will be ready for the next stage.

Racking

When fermentation is completely finished, the wine must be removed from the sediment of dead and living yeast cells, particles of pulp, protein, enzymes, bicarbonates, tartrates, and so on. Failure to do this results in an undrinkable wine smelling and tasting or rotting vegetation.

The simplest way to remove the clearing wine from the sediment is to siphon it off, commonly called 'racking' the wine. Never pour the wine out through the bung-hole. Place the jar to be emptied on a table and the jar to be filled on the floor. Insert one end of the siphon into the wine and, if you wish, fix it firmly with the aid of a bored bung cut into two through the diameter of the bored hole. A narrow additional vent hole is needed so that air can replace the wine as it is removed.

Place the halves of the bung around the siphon tube and fit the bung and tube into the neck of the jar. Push the tube to the appropriate level, suck the other end to fill it with wine, then place that end into the jar on the floor. The wine will flow steadily until the upper jar is emptied. By careful tilting of the upper jar, almost all the wine can be removed without disturbing the sediment. Or use a J-tube or blocked-end siphon. Top the clean jar up with wine

Racking off wine into another container removes it from the sediment at the bottom of the fermentation jar.

from the excess bottle, add a Campden tablet, bung tight, label and store in a cool place.

If the racking has been well done there will be nothing but sediment in the fermentation jar. This must be discarded and the jar washed out, drained dry and put away. Similarly the wine from the excess bottle can be poured or siphoned into a smaller bottle and that sediment can also be washed out. If the racking has left some wine in the jar it can all be poured into the bottle. Replace the cotton wool plug and stand the bottle in the refrigerator. After a few days the wine will be clear and can be transferred to a clean bottle.

Filtering and fining

Should the wine remain hazy after a few months, proprietary wine finings may be added. Remove some of the wine from the jar and slowly pour it into the finings, stirring well all the time. When the finings are well mixed in, return the wine to the jar and stir well to distribute the finings evenly throughout the wine. Replace the bung and leave the jar in a cool place for a few days or a week. Alternatively a proprietary filter can be used. These are efficient and simple to use and full instructions are supplied with them. As soon as the wine is clear, rack it from the sediment, top up the jar, bung tight and store until you have time for bottling.

Bottling

Bottling can be done once the wine is completely clear. Do not be disappointed if you find the flavour of the wine at this stage is lacking; it may well taste 'yeasty'. The flavour and aroma of the wine will improve as it is stored, most country wines will need at least six months from when they are made, some up to three years to mature sufficiently. You can only tell by experience and actually tasting the wine. Remember with red wine to always use brown or green bottles to preserve the colour.

For each 4.5 L (1 gal) of wine you will need six sterilized bottles and corks. Siphon the wine into them, fit corks, label the bottles and again store flat to keep the corks moist.

Other wines

Sherry-type wines. Sherry-type wines are matured slightly differently from other types of wine. They must be stored in jars about seven-eighths full that are plugged with cotton wool rather than with a bung. The plug filters out any microbes but permits the entry of air into the head-space above the maturing wine. Ferment on as strong as possible so that the alcohol content of the wine is appropriate to the oxidation necessary to obtain the characteristic nutty sherry flavour. Sherry-type wines are best matured dry and sweetened subsequently if so desired.

Sparkling wines. Sparkling wines are best made from a light-flavoured still wine that is also light in alcohol – say, 10 to 11%. When the wine is clear and about six months old, rack it into a clean jar and stir in 70 g (2½ oz) of caster sugar per 4.5 L (1 gal). (This quantity is critical and should not be exceeded or reduced.) Next, add an activated Champagne wine yeast and a little nutrient. Finally, fit an airlock and move the jar to a warm position for a few hours until the wine can clearly be see to be fermenting normally.

Wash and sterilize six sparkling wine bottles (no others are suitable since they may be unsafe due to the pressure that builds up in the bottle) and pour the fermenting wine into the bottles, leaving a headspace of 5 cm (2 in). Fit a softened, hollow-domed plastic stopper or a blister stopper to each bottle and wire it on with a cage. Leave the bottle on its side in a warm room, say 20°C (68°F) for one week while the sugar is fermented, then move it to a cool place and keep it for at least six months, preferably longer, before disgorging the sediment.

Sediment will have deposited along the bottom side of the bottle, and this must be shaken down into the stopper or blister. To do this, place the bottles, head first, into a bottle carton set at an angle of 45 degrees. Each day, give the bottles a slight shake and twist, slowly moving the bottle round and round until the sediment has settled in the stopper or blister.

Make up a solution of one dozen ice cubes, well crushed, and 30 ml (2 tbsn) of cooking salt. Stand the bottles, head down, in the ice for about 10 minutes to freeze the wine and the sediment in the stopper. Remove the cage, extract the stopper, quickly add one or two saccharin pellets and insert a clean and softened stopper. Replace the cage and store the wine for a few weeks or months longer. It helps if the wine in the bottle is first chilled (upside down, of course) for some hours in the refrigerator, since this inhibits the release of the carbon dioxide. It also helps if you remember to handle the bottle carefully without shaking it and disturbing the level of carbon dioxide.

If blister stoppers have been used, seal the blisters with the wires provided and bend them down in accordance with the instructions.

Gooseberries, pears, rhubarb, white currants, and elderflowers all make splendid sparkling wines using this method.

Fortified wines. Port or sherry-type wines can be fortified with additional spirit at the end of fermentation, after it has been racked and when the wine is bright. Vodka is the best spirit to add since it is colourless and tasteless, and will not affect the flavour of the wine.

Blending No matter how much care you take in making wine, occasionally the result is not quite as pleasing as you would like it to be. There may be nothing wrong with the wine itself but perhaps the fruit was too sour, or maybe insufficient acid was added to a flower must, or perhaps the wine is too sweet, or the flavour simply lacks appeal. Do not throw away such wines. As long as the smell and taste is clean and free from infection, then the wine can be blended with another. Almost all commercial grape wines are blended to harmonize the flavour.

Blending emphasizes the best in wines and diminishes the worst. Bland wines develop character and new flavours are created. Simply pour the wines to be blended into a large bin, give them a gentle stir and return the blended wine to the jars. Sometimes fermentation starts again, so it is as well to fit an airlock to each jar after the wines have been blended. A new deposit is often thrown as well. Leave the blend for about a month to homogenize, then bottle it and think of a suitable name to describe it. All wines blend with one another. Sometimes a thin, flower wine can greatly improve a vegetable wine.

Wine Troubleshooting

All these faults can be avoided by: proper sterilization of equipment and ingredients, the right adjustment of additives, using Campden tablets to suppress bacteria and wild yeasts, and the addition of a vigorous wine yeast starter.

FAULT	CAUSE
Fermentation of must will not start	Must too cold
	Must too hot
	Yeast added too soon after Campden tablets or depectinizer
Fermentation stops too soon	Too cold
	Yeast action stopped by high alcohol content
	Yeast action stopped by too much sugar. Lack of yeast nutrient or acid
Fermentation will not stop	Yeast not worked out
Lacks character	Insufficient tannin
Lacks bouquet and flavour	Insufficient acid
Wine turns acid (vinegar)	Vinegar fly or bacteria has got into the wine
Yeasty flavour	Probably too much yeast
'Off' flavours	Too long between racking, leaving lees in wine
Rotten cabbage smell	Leaving wine on sediment for too long
Geranium smell	Using potassium sorbate to terminate fermentation and not sterilizing
Bitter almond smell	Prussic acid from fruit stones
Wine is hazy	Pectin haze, pectin destroying enzyme not used
	Starch haze caused by unripe fruit or cereal
	Suspended particles in the wine
Oiliness or ropiness	Lactic acid bacteria
Moulds	Micro-organisms

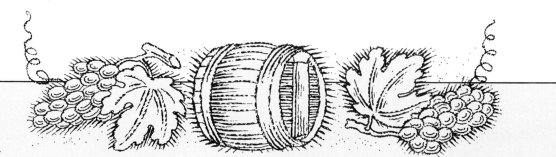

REMEDY

Raise temperature to 21°–25.5°C (70°–78°F)

Cool and put in some more yeast. Overheating kills the yeast. Some yeasts can take a week to start. If nothing has happened after a week, add a teaspoon of granulated baker's yeast or reduce the sugar by diluting the must with warm water, then add a fresh batch of yeast

If Campden tablets or depectinizers are added to a must, a day should elapse before the yeast is added. Wait, then add a fresh batch of yeast

Raise temperature

Mix fresh yeast in a starter bottle. Add to this 568 ml (1 pt) of the wine. When fermentation restarts add the rest of the wine, 568 ml (1 pt) at a time, wait for fermentation to continue before adding the next amount

Try above method, but add yeast nutrient and acid. Or double the amount of water and start again

Add Campden tablets to stop the action of the yeast. White wines can re-start fermentation in hot weather

Add 5 ml (1 tsp) grape tannin powder or liquid to 4.5 L (1 gal) of wine

If wine is sound, blend it with another wine with a too pronounced smell and taste

None – throw it away and start again. Use sound fruit and keep the fermentation vessel covered during aerobic fermentation and sealed with an airlock while fermenting. Add Campden tablets with the must and for storage

Leave to store for two or three months. It will cure itself in time

Rack when fermentation has finished and every eight weeks as sediment forms

Nothing can be done, discard the wine and sterilize the jar

Add one Campden tablet to 4.5 L (1 gal) of wine when adding potassium sorbate

No known remedy. Exclude all large stones from the must and do not crack small pips and seeds

When fruit has a lot of pectin, a pectin destroying enzyme should be added before fermentation

These hazes are difficult to remove but filtering and fining helps or try using Bentonite. Always use a cereal yeast for cereal wines

These particles can normally be filtered out

Wine goes thick and looks like egg white. Beat wine into a froth and add two Campden tablets per 4.5 L (1 gal) of wine. The taste is not affected

Occasionally caused when fermentation is slow in starting or if utensils are not properly sterilized. Skim off mould and add a Campden tablet. After a day add more yeast

Storing and Serving Wine

Having taken great pains to produce excellent wines, it would be a pity to spoil them by not serving them to their best advantage. Most home winemakers serve their wines far too young. Anxious to taste them, they often drink them long before they are adequately mature. Some wines develop quickly and are at their best when still young and fresh, but most wines need a period of maturity in bulk and another in the bottle. Wines that are light in alcohol, body and flavour usually develop most quickly and are often ready for drinking some three months after making them. This applies especially to some flower wines and to wines made from canned fruit and fruit juices. The wine made from concentrates can be ready in six to eight weeks. Instant wines can be drunk after only three to six weeks. Stronger wines with higher proportions of fruit ingredients, acids, tannin and alcohol, take anything from one to three years to mature.

If you find it impossible to resist the temptation to taste your country wines early, then try bottling them in half-size bottles or at least in some half-size bottles and some full-size bottles. By opening the half-size bottles at monthly intervals you will be able to monitor the progress of the wine and still have some full-size bottles left when the wine is mature and at its best. It will keep for several

A full-bodied red wine can be a very pleasant accompaniment to the cheese course in a meal.

years, at least, so there is no hurry to drink it from fear of losing it. Instant wine, can be drunk almost immediately.

Storing

Wine should be stored in a cool, dark, dry place which is well ventilated with a temperature of 7°–10°C (45°–50°F). If you are using straight-sided corks and the bottles are to be stored for a while they must be laid flat so that the cork stays wet and slightly swollen to maintain a seal. The bottles also need to be kept in wine racks. Bottles with plastic stoppers can be kept upright.

If you have stored your wine in a large container, it should be emptied within a week of opening or the wine may turn sour.

Decanting

When you take your wine from store, check to see if there is any sediment – there usually is. If so, the wine should be decanted before serving. This means to pour off the clear wine into another bottle, decanter or carafe without disturbing the sediment at the bottom of the bottle. This is not too difficult to do if the bottle is emptied in one, steady pouring and is not tipped too high.

Serving

As discussed previously, wines belong to certain categories: aperitif, table, dessert, sparkling and also social. When to serve them is usually determined by whether they are dry or sweet.

Most wines taste best when served with appropriate food, although some taste best on their own (see page 10). Light wines with lightly-flavoured food and more robust wines with more strongly-flavoured foods is a good rule of thumb. Use wine in cooking too — one glassful is usually enough. Marinate meat and fish in dry wines (red or white), add sweet wines to fresh fruits. Use white wine instead of water when stewing fruit. For cooking purposes, it is sufficient to pour the ends of bottles into one bottle reserved exclusively for culinary use.

Once you have made your choice, prepare the wine carefully. Sparkling wines, white table wines and rosé wines, all taste much better when served chilled. Red wines, however, are best at room temperature. But this temperature varies at different times of the year — around 20°C (68°F) is thought to be the ideal. In very cold weather, red wines may have to be warmed slightly and this is best done by leaving the bottle in a warm room for a day or two, so that it can acclimatize gradually. White wines may be chilled in the refrigerator for two hours or placed in a bucket of iced water for a quarter of an hour. The right temperature makes a significant difference to the taste and flavour of a wine.

The wine should also be served in suitable glasses. A wine glass should be colourless and undecorated in any way, and should have a stem firmly attached to a foot or base and supporting an incurved bowl. White, rosé and sparkling wines show up best in a tulip-shaped glass, while red wines look best in a more rounded shape as this helps to hold in the bouquet and prevent it from escaping. Fill the glasses to between a half and two-thirds of their capacity, to leave room for the bouquet to develop on top of the wine.

The quality of homemade wines
When drinking your wines, check their clarity and colour and savour the bouquet. Next take a mouthful of wine, chew it slowly, swallow and appreciate the flavour.

Obviously, it is not possible to make wines to equal the great vintages of France, Germany, Spain or Portugal, but comparable table wines can be made. The following chart will help you to analyze the quality of your wines, once you have set some kind of standard in your mind.

The country wines tend to have a strong aroma from the ingredients used, but there is no reason why they cannot compare well with wines made from grapes. The flavour will be different but not the quality.

Wine Quality Chart

Sight

Clarity:
Star bright, clear, dull, veiled, deposit

Colour – White:
Colourless, greenish, pale yellow, straw, gold, amber

Rosé:
Watery pink, pale pink, pretty pink, orange brown

Red:
Black-red, deep red, ruby, light red, blue-red, brown-red

Overall:
Excellent, very good, good, fair, poor

Smell

Aroma:
Fruity, flowery, spicy, vinous, other

Bouquet:
None, slight, clean, pleasant, full, rich

General:
Yeasty, vinegarish, mouldy, infected, peardrops

Overall:
Excellent, very good, good, fair, poor

Taste

Sweetness:
Very sweet, sweet, medium sweet, medium dry, dry, very dry

Acidity:
Sharp, pleasant, bland, medicinal

Tannin:
Soft, firm, hard, astringent

Body:
Thin, light, medium, full, heavy

Flavour:
Delicate, pleasant, pronounced, off, foul

Overall:
Excellent, very good, good, fair, poor

Chapter 3
A–Z
of
Wine Recipes

Fruit, vegetables and flowers have long been used by the country winemaker to produce full-flavoured wines. Herbs, grains and spices can also make satisfying wines providing natural additives are included. Grape wines can be made from fresh, dried or concentrated grape juice or can be added to other wines to give body and flavour. Blending is common practice in all winemaking and many country wines can be improved by using a mixture of different fruits. All the recipes contain clear, detailed instructions but the earlier chapters of the book should be thoroughly read and understood before a recipe is embarked on.

Almond and Raisin Wine

Yield: 6 bottles

Classification: Dessert, sweet, white

57 g (2 oz) almonds
450 g (1 lb) raisins
3 lemons
4.5 L (1 gal) water
1.35 kg (3 lb) light brown sugar
Tannin
All-purpose yeast and nutrient
Campden tablets

Sterilize all equipment as needed and start your records.

Blanch the almonds by soaking in very hot water for a few minutes. Pare the lemons avoiding all white pith and express and strain the juice. Chop the almonds and raisins, deseeding if necessary. Simmer in 4.5 L (1 gal) of water for 1 hour.

Strain into a polythene bin and make up the liquid to 4.5 L (1 gal). Add the sugar and stir until dissolved; then add the lemon rind and juice, the tannin, yeast and the nutrient.

Cover the bin and stand it in a warm place and leave to ferment on the pulp for 14 days, stirring daily. At the end of this period, strain the must into a fermentation jar and fit an airlock. Ferment out at around 16°C (61°F).

When fermentation is complete, rack the wine into a clean jar, add 1 crushed Campden tablet and close with a bung or safety lock. Rack every two months till clear, then bottle. Ideally, leave to mature for 1–2 years.

Apple Wine

Yield: 6 to 7 bottles

Classification: Table, dry, white

*4 kg (9 lb) mixed cooking and eating apples
5 ml (1 tsp) pectic enzyme
Campden tablets
5 ml (1 tsp) citric acid
4.5 L (1 gal) water
2.5 ml (½ tsp) grape tannin (optional)
Champagne wine yeast and nutrient
700–900 g (1½–2 lb) white sugar*

Sterilize all equipment as needed and start your records.

Wash and crush the apples, or cut them into small pieces with a stainless steel knife. Remove and discard all bruised portions and maggot holes. Leave on the skin and core provided the pips are not broken or cut.

Drop the prepared apples into a mashing bin containing the pectic enzyme, 1 crushed Campden tablet, the citric acid and the water. Cover and leave for 24 hours. Next day, check the specific gravity, add the tannin, and activated yeast and nutrient. Ferment on the pulp for 5 days, keeping the fruit submerged.

Strain out the juice and press the apples dry, preferably in a fruit press. Discard the pulp. Stir in the sugar. Pour the must into a fermentation jar and any excess into a bottle. Fit an airlock to the jar and a plug of cotton wool to the neck of the bottle. Ferment out at a temperature of around 16°C (61°F).

Siphon the clearing wine into a sterilized jar, add 1 crushed Campden tablet, top up with wine from the bottle, bung tight, label and store until clear (about 8 weeks). If the wine is slow to clear, 30 ml (2 tbsn) of fresh milk, well mixed in, soon precipitates the haze. When the wine is bright, rack again and keep for at least 9 months before bottling. Bottle, seal and label.

Keep for 3 to 4 months before serving.

Variations: You can make an attractive deep rosé wine by including 900 g (2 lb) of blackberries, 450 g (1 lb) elderberries, or 900 g (2 lb) stoned black plums or damsons. Wash, crush and add them to the apples at the very outset.

An attractive rosé wine can be made by adding some blackberries to the basic Apple Wine recipe.

Apricot (dried) Wine

Yield: 6 bottles

Classification: Dessert, sweet, golden

450 g (1 lb) dried apricots
Water
450 g (1 lb) raisins
1.35 kg (3 lb) light brown sugar
7 g (¼ oz) citric acid
2.5 ml (½ tsp) grape tannin
All-purpose yeast and nutrient
Campden tablets
5 ml (1 tsp) pectin enzyme

Sterilize all equipment as needed and start your records.

Wash the apricots, cut them up and soak them for 12 hours in enough cold water to cover the fruit. Wash and chop the raisins and deseed if necessary. Place them, with the apricots and the water in which they have soaked, into a polythene bin. Thoroughly dissolve the sugar in a little hot water and add this to the bin, together with the pectin enzyme.

Add the tannin and citric acid and stir thoroughly, then add enough hot water to make up to 4.5 L (1 gal). After 24 hours, add the yeast and nutrient. Cover the bin and stand it in a warm place. Leave to ferment on the pulp for eight days, stirring daily. Strain the must into a fermentation jar, discard the pulp, and seal with an airlock. Ferment out at around 16°C (61°F).

When fermentation is complete, rack into a clean jar, add 1 crushed Campden tablet and close with a bung or safety lock. Rack every two months till clear, then bottle. Ideally, leave to mature for 1–2 years. This wine is also an excellent base for Apricot liqueur.

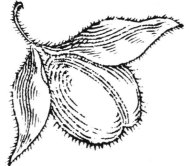

Balm Wine

Yield: 6 bottles

Classification: Social, medium, white

2.25 L (4 pt) fresh balm leaves
2 lemons
450 g (1 lb) sultanas
4.5 L (1 gal) water
All-purpose yeast and nutrient
1 kg (2¼ lb) white sugar
Campden tablets

Sterilize all equipment as needed and start your records.

Wash the fresh (wild or cultivated) leaves in water, chop them up and put them into a boiling pan. Thinly pare the lemon rinds, avoiding all white pith. Express and strain the juice, wash and chop the sultanas.

Bring the water, balm leaves and lemon parings to the boil. Simmer for 10 minutes, then strain into a bin containing the sultanas. Discard the herbs and parings, top up with cold water and, when cool, add the lemon juice and the activated wine yeast and nutrient. Cover loosely and ferment for 5 days.

Strain out, press and discard the sultanas. Stir in the sugar. Pour the must into a fermentation jar and any excess into a bottle. Fit an airlock to the jar and a plug of cotton wool into the neck of the bottle. Ferment out at around 18°C (64°F).

Siphon the clearing wine into a clean jar, add 1 crushed Campden tablet, top up with wine from the bottle, bung tight and label. Store for 3 months before bottling.

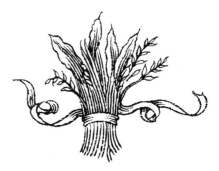

Balm leaves, picked in the wild or cultivated in the garden, can be used to make a medium white wine.

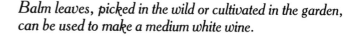

Banana Wine

Yield: 6 bottles

Classification: Dessert, sweet, white

1.8 kg (4 lb) old, ripe bananas
5.7 L (1¼ gal) water
115 g (4 oz) raisins
1 orange
1 lemon
1.35 kg (3 lb) sugar
14 g (½ oz) citric acid
2.5 ml (½ tsp) grape tannin
All-purpose yeast and nutrient
Campden tablets

Sterilize all equipment as needed and start your records.

Peel the bananas, retaining about 225 g (½ lb) of their skins. Put the bananas and skins in a nylon bag, place it in a large pan or boiler with 5.7 L (1¼ gal) of water and simmer for ½ an hour. Express and strain the juice from the orange and lemon.

Place the sugar, orange and lemon juice, chopped deseeded raisins, tannin and citric acid in a polythene bin. Pour the liquid from the bananas into the bin and stir until the sugar is fully dissolved.

When cool, squeeze as much juice as possible from the bag into the bin. Add the yeast and yeast nutrient. Cover the bin, stand in a warm place and ferment on the pulp for 7 days, stirring daily.

Strain out the must into a fermentation jar, discard the pulp, and close it with an airlock. Ferment out at around 16°C (61°F).

When fermentation is complete, rack into a clean jar, add one crushed Campden tablet and close with a bung or safety lock. Rack every two months till clear, then bottle. Ideally, leave for 1–2 years to mature.

Barley Wine

Yield: 7 bottles

Classification: Dessert, sweet, golden

450 g (1 lb) old potatoes
2 lemons
450 g (1 lb) raisins
450 g (1 lb) crushed, flaked or pearl barley
4.5 L (1 gal) boiling water
115 g (¼ lb) diastatic malt syrup
Cereal wine yeast and nutrient
1.35 kg (3 lb) Demerara sugar
Tokay wine yeast and nutrient
Campden tablets

Sterilize all equipment as needed and start your records.

Make this wine during the winter when main crop potatoes are old but not seeding. Scrub them thoroughly, cut them up into dice-sized pieces or thin slices. Thinly pare the lemons, avoiding all white pith, and express and strain the juice. Wash and chop the raisins.

Put the potatoes into a bin with the barley, lemon rind and raisins. Pour over the boiling water, cover and leave to cool. Meanwhile, dilute the malt syrup with an additional cupful of tepid water in a bowl, add the cereal yeast and beat in plenty of air. Leave until the barley must is cool.

Add the barley must mixture and lemon juice to the bin and stir well. Cover loosely and ferment on the pulp for 7 days, keeping the pulp submerged. Strain out, press and discard the pulp. Stir in one-third of the sugar. Pour the must into a fermentation jar and any excess into a bottle. Fit an airlock to the jar and plug the neck of the bottle with cotton wool. Ferment for 1 week.

Remove half the wine from the jar and stir in another third of the sugar. When it is completely dissolved, add the activated Tokay yeast and return the wine to the jar and any excess to the bottle. After a further week, again remove half the wine from the jar, stir in the last of the sugar and, when it is dissolved, return it to the jar and the excess to the bottle. Leave the wine until fermentation is finished, then siphon the clearing wine off the sediment into a clean jar. Top up from the bottle, add 1 crushed Campden tablet, bung tight, label and store the wine until it is bright.

The wine and sediment left in the jar may be poured into the bottle and left in a cool place until the sediment settles. The clear wine should then be transferred to another bottle and the sediment discarded. This wine can

Barley and Raisin Wine

Yield: 6 bottles

Classification: Table, medium, white

450 g (1 lb) whole barley grains
450 g (1 lb) raisins
450 g (1 lb) potatoes
1.60 kg (3½ lb) sugar
10 ml (2 tsp) citric acid
2.5 ml (½ tsp) grape tannin
Cereal wine yeast and nutrient
Campden tablets

Sterilize all equipment as needed and start your records.

Soak the barley in water overnight. Peel and chop up the potatoes. Deseed the raisins, if necessary, mix them with the barley and put the mixture through a mincer or grinder. Put the chopped potatoes, minced barley and raisins and sugar in a polythene bin. Heat sufficient water, to cover the bin, to almost boiling point and pour in. Add the citric acid and tannin. Add crushed Campden tablet, then cover the bin. After 24 hours, add the yeast and nutrient and place the bin in a warm place to ferment.

Leave for 10 days, stirring daily. Strain the liquid into a fermentation jar, discard the pulp, and make it up to 4.5 L (1 gal) and fit an airlock. Ferment out at around 16°C (61°F).

When fermentation is complete, rack into a clean jar, add 1 crushed Campden tablet and close the jar with a bung or safety lock. Rack every two months till clear, then bottle. Ideally, leave for 1–2 years to mature.

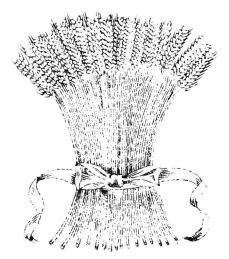

Wholegrain, flaked or ground barley can be easily obtained for making barley wines.

be used for topping up the jar after racking off.

Store in bulk for at least 2 years, then bottle and keep for a further year or more. It does not really begin to be enjoyable until it is at least 3 years old but by then it is very smooth indeed.

Beetroot Wine

Yield: 6 to 6½ bottles

Classification: Dessert, sweet, red

2.25 kg (5 lb) beetroots
3 large lemons
450 g (1 lb) raisins
4.5 L (1 gal) water
Port wine yeast and nutrient
1.35 kg (3 lb) sugar
Campden tablets

Sterilize all equipment as needed and start your records.

Choose freshly dug beetroots. Trim them, scrub them clean and cut into small, dice-sized pieces. Thinly pare the lemon rinds, avoiding all white pith. Express and strain the lemon juice and set it aside. Wash and chop the raisins.

Place the beetroot in a boiling pan with the lemon rinds. Add enough water comfortably to fill the pan, cover it, bring to the boil and simmer for up to 1½ hours until the beetroot is soft to the fork. Strain the liquor through a nylon strainer or bag into a polythene bin containing the raisins. Top up to the required level, cover the bin and leave the liquor to cool. Then measure the specific gravity and add the lemon juice and activated yeast and nutrient.

Ferment on the raisin pulp for 5 days, keeping the raisins submerged. Strain out, press and discard the raisins. Stir in one-third of the sugar and fit an airlock. Ferment for about 7 days. Remove half the wine, stir in another third of the sugar and return the fermenting must to the jar and the accompanying bottle. About a week later, repeat the process with the last of the sugar and continue the fermentation.

Siphon the clearing wine off the sediment into a clean jar and top up with the wine from the bottle. Add 1 crushed Campden tablet, bung tight, label and store. Pour the residue from the jar into the bottle and, as soon as the sediment settles, pour the clean wine into another bottle that it can just fill.

Mature this wine for 1 year in bulk. Bottle and store for another 1 year before drinking.

Beetroot wine is a sweet red wine that can be drunk with the dessert course of a meal.

Birch Sap Wine

Yield: 6 bottles

Classification: Table, dry, white

4 L (7 pt) fresh birch sap
2 lemons
225 g (½ lb) raisins
All-purpose wine yeast and nutrient
150 ml (5 fl oz) cold tea (optional)
900 g (2 lb) white sugar
Campden tablets

Sterilize all equipment as needed and start your records.

Thinly pare the lemons, avoiding all white pith. Express and strain the juice, wash and chop the raisins.

Simmer together the sap, lemon rinds and juice for 20 minutes, skimming off any scum that rises. Strain the hot liquid onto the raisins, cover and leave to cool. Add the activated yeast and nutrient, and if using, the cold tea. Ferment on the fruit for 5 days keeping the vessel covered.

Strain out and press the raisins dry. Stir in the sugar. Pour the must into a sterilized fermentation jar and fit an airlock. Ferment out in a steady warm place. When fermentation is finished, move the jar to a cool place for a few days. Siphon the clearing wine into a sterilized storage jar, add 1 crushed Campden tablet, top up with cold boiled water and bung tight. Label and leave until bright then rack again.

Keep for 6 months before bottling.

Note: Saps lack acid and tannin and so the inclusion of some lemon juice is essential to a good fermentation and to a pleasant smell and taste. Half a cup of cold tea added to the must would improve its character still more.

Variations: *Sycamore tree sap* and *Walnut tree sap* wines can be made in the same way (see page 18).

Sap wines used to be popular in the past but are not made very often today. Mature birch trees are best tapped on a fine cold morning in spring. Drill a hole in the trunk about 50 cm (20 in) from the ground and about 2.5–3 cm (1–1¼ in) deep with a diameter of 1 cm (⁴/₁₀ in). Push a plastic tube gently into the hole, but not too far. Place the other end of the tube into a sterilized jar with a crushed Campden tablet and plug with cotton wool. The flow of sap can take a few hours or even a day to reach the required 4 L (7 pt). Take the tube from the tree and plug the hole with some dowel rod and cover the end with candle wax.

Blackberry Wine

Yield: 6 to 7 bottles

Classification: Dessert, sweet, red

2.7 kg (6 lb) blackberries
350 g (¾ lb) raisins
4.5 L (1 gal) water
5 ml (1 tsp) pectic enzyme
Campden tablets
10 ml (2 tsp) citric acid
2.5 ml (½ tsp) grape tannin
Port wine yeast and nutrient
1.35 kg (3 lb) white sugar

Sterilize all equipment as needed and start your records.

Stalk, wash and crush the berries. Wash and chop the raisins. Place the prepared berries and the water in a suitable container and heat to 85°C (176°F). Maintain the temperature for 15 minutes, then leave to cool. Strain out the berry pulp through fine-meshed nylon bag and press the fruit dry. Discard the pulp. Add the raisins, the pectic enzyme, 1 crushed Campden tablet and the citric acid. Cover and leave for 24 hours.

Next day, check the specific gravity, add the tannin and activated yeast and nutrient. Ferment on the raisin pulp for 5 days keeping the raisins submerged.

Strain out the juice and press the raisins dry. Discard the raisin pulp. Stir in one-third of the sugar, pour the must into a fermentation jar and a bottle. Fit an airlock to the jar and a plug of cotton wool to the bottle and continue the fermentation. Stir in half the remaining sugar 1 week later and repeat the process with the last of the sugar after a further week – then leave to ferment out.

Siphon the clearing wine into a sterilized jar, add 1 crushed Campden tablet, top up with wine from the bottle, bung tight, label and store. As soon as the wine is bright, rack again.

Store this wine in bulk for at least 1 year and preferably 2. Then bottle and store for a further 6 months. If you wish, you can sweeten the finished wine to your taste when decanting just before serving.

Variations: You can make this wine into a dry table wine by reducing the quantity of fruit and sugar by one-third and the acid by one-half. Make it in the same way but bottle when the wine is a year old.

Bilberries and blueberries, if available, may also be blended with blackberries.

Blackcurrant Wine

Yield: 6 to 7 bottles

Classification: Social, dry, red

*1.35 kg (3 lb) blackcurrants
225 g (½ lb) raisins
4.5 L (1 gal) water
1.35 kg (3 lb) white sugar
Burgundy wine yeast and nutrient
Campden tablets*

Sterilize all equipment as needed and start your records.

Stalk, wash and crush the blackcurrants. Wash and chop the raisins. Place the prepared blackcurrants and the water in a suitable container and heat to 85°C (176°F). Maintain the temperature for 15 minutes, then leave to cool.

Strain out the currant pulp through a fine-meshed nylon bag. Discard the pulp. Add the raisins and stir the sugar into the juice until it is dissolved. Add the activated yeast and nutrient and pour the must into a fermentation jar and any excess into a bottle. Fit the airlock into the jar and plug the bottle with cotton wool. Ferment out at around 21°C (70°F).

Siphon the clearing wine into a sterilized jar, add 1 crushed Campden tablet, bung tight, label and store until the wine is bright, then rack again.

Mature this wine in bulk for 1 year before bottling. Bottle and store for a further 6 months before drinking.

Burgundy Wine (instant)

Yield: 6 bottles

Classification: Table, dry, red

*1 can, 1 kg (2¼ lb) Burgundy grape juice concentrate
Water
225 g (½ lb) white sugar
Granulated yeast and nutrient
Campden tablets*

Sterilize all equipment as needed and start your records.

Pour the concentrate into a jug, rinsing out any juice from the can with very hot water. Pour the contents of the jug into the fermentation jar, then add warm water to make up 3.4 L (6 pt).

Dissolve half of the sugar in warm water and add this to the jar; stir well, then add the yeast and nutrient, and seal the jar with an airlock.

Stand the jar in a warm place, about 21°C (70°F), maintaining this temperature. After three days, add half of the remaining sugar, dissolved. After a further 3 days, add the remaining 57 g (2 oz) of sugar, dissolved and make the total quantity of must up to 4.5 L (1 gal) with warm water.

Fermentation should finish in 14 to 21 days from commencement; when finished, rack off the wine into a clean jar and add 1 crushed Campden tablet. Stand the wine for one week, then filter it repeatedly until clear and then bottle. This wine can be drunk within two weeks of clearing.

A Burgundy wine is one of the most pleasant red wines to drink on its own or with a meal.

Carrot Wine

Yield: 6 to 6½ bottles

Classification: Table, dry, white

2 kg (4½ lb) carrots
2 oranges
2 lemons
225 g (½ lb) sultanas
4.5 L (1 gal) water
1 kg (2¼ lb) white sugar
Burgundy wine yeast and nutrient
Campden tablets

Sterilize all equipment as needed and start your records.

Select good quality, freshly dug, main crop carrots. Wash, scrub and dice them. Thinly pare the oranges and lemons, avoiding all white pith. Express and strain the juice and set aside. Wash and chop the sultanas.

Boil the carrots, citrus rinds and water together for 30 minutes. Strain the liquor through a nylon strainer, into a polythene bin containing the sultanas. Stir well, top up with cold water and cover the bin until the liquor is cool. Then add the lemon and orange juice and the activated yeast and nutrient. Cover the bin and ferment on the sultana pulp for 3 days.

Strain out the sultanas, stir in the sugar and pour the must into a sterilized fermentation jar. Fit the airlock and ferment out.

Siphon the clearing wine off the sediment into a clean jar and top up with the wine from the bottle. Add 1 crushed Campden tablet, bung tight, label and store. Pour the residue from the jar into the bottle and, as soon as the sediment settles, pour the clean wine into another bottle that it can just fill.

Mature for 1 year in bulk. Bottle and store for another year before drinking.

Celery Wine

Yield: 6 to 6½ bottles

Classification: Table, medium, white

2 kg (4½ lb) celery
2 lemons
225 g (½ lb) sultanas
4.5 L (1 gal) water
1 kg (2¼ lb) sugar
Burgundy wine yeast and nutrient
Campden tablets

Sterilize all equipment as needed and start your records.

Select large celeries in good condition. Cut off the leaves and roots, remove the stalks, wash them thoroughly and cut them into small pieces. Thinly pare the lemons, avoiding all white pith. Express and strain the juice and set aside. Wash and chop the sultanas.

Boil the celery, lemon parings and water together for 45 minutes. Strain out the liquor through a nylon strainer or bag into a polythene bin containing the sultanas. Top up to the required level, cover the bin and leave the liquor to cool. Then measure the specific gravity and add the lemon juice and activated yeast and nutrient.

Ferment on the sultana pulp for 5 days, keeping the sultanas submerged. Strain out, press and discard the sultanas. Stir in one-third of the sugar and fit an airlock. Ferment for about 7 days. Remove half the wine, stir in another third of the sugar and return the fermenting must to the jar and the accompanying bottle. About a week later, repeat the process with the last of the sugar and continue the fermentation. Siphon the clearing wine off the sediment into a clean jar and top up with the wine from the bottle. Add 1 crushed Campden tablet, bung tight, label and store. Pour the residue from the jar into the bottle and, as soon as the sediment settles, pour the clean wine into another bottle that it can just fill.

Keep for at least 1 year before drinking.

Vegetables can make very different wines: Carrot Wine is a dry, white wine and Parsnip Wine (page 75) is a sweet, golden dessert wine.

Cherry Wine

Yield: 6 to 7 bottles

Classification: Social, sweet, red

2.25 kg (5 lb) cooking and Morello cherries, mixed
4.5 L (1 gal) water
1.35 kg (3 lb) white sugar
Burgundy wine yeast and nutrient
Campden tablets

Sterilize all equipment as needed and start your records. Wash, stalk and stone the cherries. This wine can be improved by adding 250 g (9 oz) of sultanas. Place the prepared cherries and the water in a suitable container and heat to 85°C (176°F). Maintain the temperature for 15 minutes, then leave to cool.

Strain out the cherry pulp through a fine-meshed nylon bag. Discard the pulp. Add the sultanas, if using, and stir the sugar into the juice until it is dissolved. Add the activated yeast and nutrient and pour the must into a fermentation jar and any excess into a bottle. Fit an airlock into the jar and plug the bottle with cotton wool. Ferment out at around 21°C (70°F).

Siphon the clearing wine into a sterilized jar, add 1

crushed Campden tablet, bung tight, label and store until the wine is bright, then rack again.

Mature this wine in bulk for 1 year before bottling. Bottle and store for a further 6 months before drinking.

Cowslip Wine

Yield: 6 bottles

Classification: Dessert, medium, white

*2 lemons
50 g (2 oz) dried cowslip flowers
4.5 L (1 gal) water
450 g (1 lb) white honey or
450 g (1 lb) sultanas
450 g (1 lb) white sugar
All-purpose wine yeast and nutrient
Campden tablets*

Sterilize all equipment as needed and start your records.

Thinly pare the lemons, avoiding all white pith, then chop the rind into small pieces. Express and strain the juice and set aside. Wash and chop the sultanas if using them.

Put the dried flowers and the lemon rind into a plastic bin and pour on the boiling water. Stir in the honey (or add the sultanas, if you are using these instead), the sugar, then cover them and leave to cool. Add the activated yeast and nutrient and the lemon juice, cover loosely and ferment for 4 days, keeping the flowers submerged.

Strain out and press the flowers, and pour the must into a fermentation jar. Fit an airlock and continue the fermentation until finished. In due course, siphon the wine into a clean jar and add 1 crushed Campden tablet. Bung tight and label.

Keep for 3 months before bottling. Add 2 saccharin tablets per bottle before serving.

Variations: Other dried flowers may be used in a similar way, as can fresh primrose flowers. Although the aroma of primrose is not quite so charming as cowslip it still makes an attractive wine. Gather 4.5 L (1 gal) of primrose flowers and continue as described for *Cowslip wine*.

Homemade Cherry Wine is a sweet red wine that is always a delight to drink on social occasions.

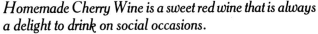

Damson Wine

Yield: 6 to 7 bottles

Classification: Social, medium, red

2 kg (4 lb) ripe damsons
4.5 L (1 gal) water
1.35 kg (3 lb) white sugar
Burgundy wine yeast and nutrient
Campden tablets

Sterilize all equipment as needed and start your records.

Wash, stalk and stone the damsons. Place the prepared damsons and the water in a suitable container and heat to 85°C (176°F). Maintain the temperature for 15 minutes, then leave to cool. Strain out the pulp through a fine-meshed nylon bag and press the fruit dry. Discard the pulp. Add 1 crushed Campden tablet and leave for 24 hours.

Next day, check the specific gravity, add the tannin and activated yeast and nutrient. Ferment for 5 days. Stir in one-third of the sugar, pour the must into a fermentation jar and a bottle. Fit an airlock to the jar and a plug of cotton wool to the bottle and continue the fermentation. Stir in half the remaining sugar 1 week later and repeat the process with the last of the sugar after a further week – then leave to ferment out.

Siphon the clearing wine into a sterilized jar, add 1 crushed Campden tablet, top up with wine from the bottle, bung tight, label and store. As soon as the wine is bright, rack again.

Variation: Add to the damsons 450 g (1 lb) washed and chopped raisins and 4 ripe bananas. Use a Port wine yeast instead of a Burgundy yeast.

Prepare the must by heat treatment and strain it on to the washed and chopped raisins. When cool, measure the specific gravity. Add the yeast and ferment on the pulp for 5 days. Strain out and press the raisins. Stir in a 5 ml (1 tsp) of citric acid, 5 ml (1 tsp) of grape tannin, and one-third of the sugar. Continue as described above.

This wine needs to be stored at least 1 year in bulk and preferably longer. It also benefits from some bottle age. When it is fully mature, it is a rich, strong, sweet after-dinner wine.

Dandelion Wine

Yield: 6 to 6½ bottles

Classification: Social, medium, white

4.5 L (1 gal) flower heads
1 orange
2 lemons
225 g (½ lb) sultanas
4.5 L (1 gal) boiling water
All-purpose wine yeast and nutrient
1 kg (2¼ lb) white sugar
Campden tablets

Sterilize all equipment as needed and start your records.

Collect the flowers and cut off the yellow heads, discarding every trace of green stem, leaf and calyx. Put the petals into a measuring jug and shake down gently: do not press. Pare the orange and lemons, making sure that all the white pith is discarded. Chop the rind. Express the juice of the orange and lemons, wash and chop the sultanas.

Put the petals into a plastic bin with the orange and lemon rinds and the sultanas. Pour over the boiling water, cover and cool. Stir in the orange and lemon juice, the activated yeast and nutrient, cover loosely and leave to ferment on the pulp for 5 days, pressing down the floating fruit and flowers twice daily.

Strain the pulp, pressing until all the juice is extracted. Discard the pulp. Stir in the sugar. Pour the must into a fermentation jar and any excess into a bottle. Fit an airlock to the fermentation jar and plug the bottle with cotton wool. Leave to ferment out at around 20°C (68°F). When fermentation is finished, move the wine to a cool place for a few days to help it to clear.

Siphon the clearing wine off the sediment into a sterilized jar. Add 1 crushed Campden tablet, top up the jar from the bottle, bung tight, label and store in a cool place. When the wine is bright, rack it again. Mature in bulk for 6 months before siphoning off into bottles.

Keep for 1 year before drinking, and sweeten to taste before serving.

Damson Wine is a medium, red wine for drinking socially, but a variation can be made with raisins and bananas that is a strong, sweet wine for drinking at the end of meals.

Date Wine

Yield: 6 to 7 bottles

Classification: Dessert, sweet, red

1 kg (2¼ lb) dates
225 g (½ lb) raisins
2 lemons
1 bitter orange
1 grapefruit
4.5 L (1 gal) boiling water
Sherry or Madeira wine yeast and nutrient
1 kg (2¼ lb) white sugar (brown for Madeira-type wine)
Campden tablets

Sterilize all equipment as needed and start your records.

Stone and chop the dates; wash and chop the raisins. Thinly pare the lemons and orange, avoiding all white pith; express and strain the lemon, orange and grapefruit juice. Chop the lemon and orange rinds finely and place them in a bin with the dates and raisins. Pour over the boiling water, cover the bin and then leave to cool.

Add the lemon, orange and grapefruit juice to the bin, together with the activated yeast and nutrient. Ferment on the pulp for 5 days, keeping the fruit submerged.

Strain out and press the fruit dry. Discard the pulp. Stir in one-third of the sugar and pour the must into a fermentation jar and any excess into a bottle. Fit an airlock to the fermentation jar and plug the neck of the bottle with cotton wool. Ferment for 7 or 8 days.

Remove some of the wine, stir in half the remaining sugar and, when it is dissolved, return it to the jar. Continue fermenting the must for a further 7 or 8 days, then stir in the last of the sugar in the same way as before and ferment out.

Move the wine to a cool place for a few days to encourage clarification, then siphon into a sterilized jar, add 1 crushed Campden tablet and top up with wine from the bottle. Bung tight, label and store for at least 1 year before bottling.

Keep this strong sweet wine for a further 6 months in bottle before drinking.

Elderberry Wine

Yield: 6 to 7 bottles

Classification: Dessert, sweet, red

2 kg (4½ lb) elderberries
450 g (1 lb) ripe bananas
450 g (1 lb) raisins
2 lemons
2 oranges
4.5 L (1 gal) water
Port wine yeast and nutrient
1.35 kg (3 lb) white sugar
Campden tablets

Sterilize all equipment as needed and start your records.

Wash and crush the elderberries. Peel and mash the bananas, wash and chop the raisins and thinly pare the rinds of the oranges and lemons, avoiding all white pith. Express and strain the citrus juice and set aside.

Put the crushed elderberries, citrus rinds, bananas, raisins and water in a boiling pan and heat to 85°C (176°F). Maintain this temperature for 15 minutes, then leave to cool. Strain into a suitable bin, pressing the fruit. Discard the pulp. Measure the specific gravity. Add the orange and lemon juice and the activated yeast and nutrient. Stir in one-third of the sugar and pour the must into a fermentation jar and a bottle. Fit an airlock to the jar and a plug of cotton wool to the bottle and continue the fermentation. Stir in half the remaining sugar 1 week later and repeat the process with the last of the sugar after a further week – then leave to ferment out.

Siphon the clearing wine into a sterilized jar, add 1 crushed Campden tablet, top up with wine from the bottle, bung tight, label and store. As soon as the wine is bright, rack again.

Store in bulk for at least 2, possibly 3, years. Bottle and store for a further 6 months before drinking.

Note: Some recipes omit the bananas and raisins but this diminishes the richness of alcohol, body, flavour and vinosity of the finished wine. Since elderberries contain no acid worth mentioning, it is important to include the citrus fruit. Heating the elderberries in the manner described extracts all the glorious colour and flavour but avoids the bitterness so often found in elderberry wines made in other ways. Ensure that it does not boil.

Elderberry Wine needs to be made carefully as boiling the fruit can spoil the flavour and colour of the wine.

Recipes

Elderflower Wine

Yield: 6 bottles

Classification: Social, medium, white

0.6 L (1 pt) elderflower blossoms
1 orange
2 lemons
225 g (½ lb) sultanas
4.5 L (1 gal) boiling water
All-purpose wine yeast and nutrient
1 kg (2¼ lb) white sugar
Campden tablets

Sterilize all equipment as needed and start your records.

Collect the elderflower heads (by severing them from the main stalks). As soon as you can, remove the blossoms from their tiny individual stems (you can use a clean comb or fork but agile fingers are more precise); it is important to ensure that no green stems are included with the blossoms since they often impart a bitterness to the wine.

Place the blossoms in a measuring jug and shake them down gently; do not press. Pare the orange and lemons, avoiding all white pith. Chop the rind and set it aside. Express and strain the juice and set aside. Wash and chop the sultanas.

Put the blooms into a plastic bin with the orange and lemon rinds, and the sultanas. Pour over the boiling water and leave to cool. Stir in the orange and lemon juice, activated yeast and nutrient, cover loosely and leave to ferment for 5 days, pressing down on the floating flowers and fruit twice daily.

Strain the must through a nylon mesh bag into a container, pressing until all the juice is extracted. Stir in the sugar. Pour the liquid into a fermentation jar and any excess into a bottle. Fit an airlock into the fermentation jar and plug the neck of the bottle with cotton wool. Leave to ferment out at a temperature of about 20°C (68°F).

When fermentation is finished, move the wine to a cool place for a few days to help it to clear. Siphon the clearing wine off the sediment into a clean jar. Add 1 crushed Campden tablet and top up the jar (if necessary) with wine from the bottle. Bung tight, label and store in a cool place until bright and clear.

Rack again, then mature in bulk for 6 months before bottling. Keep for 1 year before drinking, and sweeten to taste before serving.

Gather elderflowers on a warm sunny day when the flowers are open to make this fragrant, medium-sweet white wine.

Ginger Wine

Yield: 6 bottles

Classification: Aperitif, sweet, white

75 g (3 oz) root ginger
3 lemons
450 g (1 lb) raisins
1.25 ml (¼ tsp) cayenne pepper
4 L (7 pt) boiling water
All-purpose wine yeast and nutrient
1.35 kg (3 lb) Demerara sugar
Campden tablets

Sterilize all equipment as needed and start your records.

Firmly bruise the ginger. Thinly pare the lemons, avoiding all white pith. Express and strain the lemon juice and set aside. Wash and chop the raisins. Put the ginger, lemon rind and raisins into a bin with the cayenne and pour on the boiling water. Stir the mixture thoroughly, then cover and leave to cool.

Add the activated wine yeast and nutrient and the lemon juice. Loosely cover the bin and ferment on the pulp for 7 days, keeping the pulp submerged. Strain out, press and discard the solids. Stir in one-third of the sugar. Pour the must into a fermentation jar any excess into a bottle. Fit an airlock to the jar and plug the neck of the bottle with cotton wool. Ferment for 1 week.

Remove half the wine from the jar and stir in another third of the sugar. After a further week, again remove half the wine from the jar, stir in the last of the sugar and, when it is dissolved, return it to the jar and the excess to the bottle. Leave the wine until fermentation is finished, then siphon the clearing wine off the sediment into a clean jar. Top up from the bottle, add 1 crushed Campden tablet, bung tight, label and store the wine until it is bright.

The wine and sediment left in the jar may be poured into the bottle and left in a cool place until the sediment settles. The clear wine should then be transferred to another bottle and the sediment discarded. The wine can be used for topping up the jar after its racking.

Store this wine in bulk for 6 months and then for a further 6 months in bottle. The wine may be coloured green with a few drops of food dye if you so wish.

Variations: Some of the sugar may be replaced with an equal quantity of honey. Three or four ripe bananas may be peeled, mashed and added to the sultanas or raisins to improve the body of the wine.

25 ml (2 tbsn) of glycerine may be stirred in at the first racking to give the wine some extra smoothness.

Gooseberry 'Champagne'

Yield: 6 bottles

Classification: Sparkling, medium, white

1.5 kg (3½ lb) green gooseberries
4.5 L (1 gal) boiling water
5 ml (1 tsp) pectic enzyme
Campden tablets
1.15 kg (2½ lb) white sugar
Champagne wine yeast and nutrient
Caster sugar

Sterilize all equipment as needed and start your records.

Trim the gooseberries, wash them and put them into a polythene bin. Pour the boiling water over the gooseberries, cover and set aside. When cool, drain off and save the water and crush the now softened gooseberries with a potato masher or something similar. Return the water, add the pectic enzyme and 1 crushed Campden tablet. Cover tightly and leave for 2 days.

Strain out and press the gooseberries dry. Measure the specific gravity. Stir in the sugar, add an activated Champagne yeast and nutrient. Pour the must into a fermentation jar and any excess into a bottle. Fit an airlock to the container and a cotton wool plug to the neck of the bottle. Ferment out at a steady temperature of around 18°C (64°F).

When fermentation is finished, move the wine to a cool place for a few days and then siphon it into sterilized containers. Bung tight and store until the wine is bright then rack again.

When the wine is about 6 months old, rack into a sterilized container and stir in exactly 70 g (2¼ oz) of caster sugar and another activated Champagne wine yeast and nutrient. Fit an airlock to the container and leave it in a warm place until the wine begins to ferment.

Carefully siphon or pour the fermenting wine into sterilized champagne bottles, leaving a 5 cm (2 in) head-space at the top of each one. Fit a softened, hollow-domed blister or stopper to each bottle and wire on. Leave the bottles, on their side, in a warm place for 1 week.

Store the bottles, on their side, in a cool place for at least 6 months before drinking. Sediment will be deposited along the bottom of the bottle sides during storage and must be shaken down into the stopper or blister for removal (see page 35).

Gooseberry Wine

Yield: 7 to 8 bottles

Classification: Table, dry, white

*1.8 kg (4 lb) just ripe gooseberries
4.5 L (1 gal) boiling water
5 ml (1 tsp) pectic enzyme
Campden tablets
1.35 kg (3 lb) white sugar
Bernkastel wine yeast and nutrient*

Sterilize all equipment as needed and start your records.

Trim the gooseberries, wash them clean and place them in a polythene bin. Pour the boiling water over the gooseberries, cover and set aside. When cool, drain off and save the water, and crush the now softened gooseberries with a potato masher or something similar. Return the water, add 5 ml (1 tsp) of pectic enzyme and 1 crushed Campden tablet. Cover tightly and leave for 2 days.

Strain out and press the gooseberries dry, discarding the pulp. Measure the specific gravity. Stir in the white sugar, and add the activated yeast and nutrient. Pour the must into a fermentation jar and any excess into another container. The total quantity will be between 5.5–6.2 L (12.5–14 pt) and should produce 7 to 8 bottles of wine. Fit an airlock to each container and ferment out at a steady temperature of around 18°C (64°F).

When fermentation is finished, move the wine to a cool place for a few days and then siphon it into sterilized containers, dividing 1 crushed Campden tablet between them. Bung tight, label and store until the wine is bright, then bottle. This wine is best bottled early rather than matured in bulk.

Store the bottles for at least 1 year before serving. As the alcohol content is about 12 per cent, this wine will keep and improve for years. If necessary, sweeten it slightly to taste before serving. One saccharin tablet per bottle should be enough.

Variations: If you wish to make a sweeter, fuller wine, use 2 kg (4½ lb) of fully ripe gooseberries and 1.5 kg (3½ lb) sugar, together with a Sauternes yeast. Alternatively (a) use 225 g (½ lb) sultanas instead of the extra sugar and sweeten to taste before serving/or (b) use 225 g (½ lb) fructose instead of the extra sugar.

Gooseberries are a very versatile fruit and can be used to make a sparkling medium-sweet champagne, a dry, white table wine or a sweeter full-bodied wine.

Grape Wine

Yield: 6 to 7 bottles

Classification: Table, dry, white

8 kg (18 lb) ripe white grapes
5 ml (1 tsp) pectic enzyme
Campden tablets
White sugar as necessary
All-purpose wine yeast and nutrient

Sterilize all equipment as needed and start your records.

Stalk, wash and crush the grapes but not the pips. Place the crushed grapes in a suitable container with the pectic enzyme and 1 crushed Campden tablet. Cover and leave for 24 hours.

Next day, strain out the grapes and press dry. Discard the pulp. Measure the specific gravity of the juice. Add sufficient sugar to bring the reading up to between 1.076 and 1.090. Stir in an activated wine yeast and nutrient. Fit an airlock and ferment out at around 16°C (61°F).

When fermentation is finished, siphon off the wine from the sediment and add 1 crushed Campden tablet. Store until bright, then rack again and leave for a total of 6 months before bottling.

Store in the bottles for 3 months.

Variations: A red wine can be made from black grapes, either by fermenting on the pulp for 14 days or, better still, by using the heat treatment as described on page 14. Cool the grapes, strain, press and discard the pulp. When the liquor is cool, add the yeast and fit an airlock. Ferment out at a temperature of 20°C (68°F). Continue as for white wine, but mature in bulk for at least 18 months before bottling.

Grapefruit Wine

Yield: 6 bottles

Classification: Table, dry, white

1 can, 538 g (1¼ lb) sweetened grapefruit juice
Water
675 g (1½ lb) sugar
Granulated wine yeast and nutrient
Campden tablets

Sterilize all equipment as needed and start your records.

Pour the juice straight into the fermentation jar. Dissolve 225 g (½ lb) of the sugar in hot water and add to the vessel. Add 3.4 L (6 pt) of water and the yeast and nutrient. Seal the jar with an airlock.

Stand the jar in a warm place, about 21°C (70°F), maintaining this temperature. After three days, add half of the remaining sugar in dissolved form. After a further three days, add the remainder of the sugar, dissolved, and make up to 4.5 L (1 gal).

When fermentation has finished, in about 21 days, rack off the wine into a clean jar and add 1 crushed Campden tablet. Stand the wine for seven days, then filter it; two or more filterings may be necessary to clear the wine, which should now be ready to drink. Bottle if desired. This wine will not keep for long; consume it within two weeks.

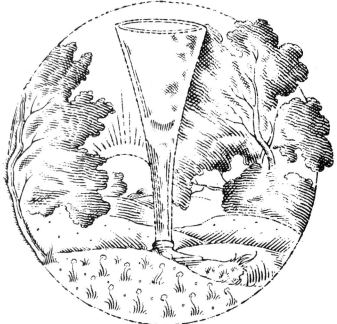

Recipes

Maize Wine

Yield: 7 bottles

Classification: Dessert, sweet, golden

675 g (1½ lb) flaked maize
4 sweet oranges
1 lemon
450 g (1 lb) sultanas or raisins
4.5 L (1 gal) boiling water
Cereal wine yeast and nutrient
1.35 kg (3 lb) Demerara sugar
Campden tablets

Sterilize all equipment as needed and start your records.

Place the flaked maize in a bin. Thinly pare the orange and lemon rinds, avoiding all white pith. Express and strain the juice. Wash and chop the sultanas.

Add the citrus rinds and sultanas to the bin and pour over the boiling water. Stir well, cover and leave to cool. Add the activated cereal wine yeast and nutrient and the orange and lemon juice. Cover loosely and ferment on the pulp for 7 days, keeping the pulp submerged.

Strain out, press and discard the pulp. Stir in one-thrid of the sugar. Pour the must into a fermentation jar and any excess into a bottle. Fit an airlock to the jar and plug the neck of the bottle with cotton wool. Ferment for 1 week.

Remove half the wine from the jar and stir in another third of the sugar. After a further week, again remove half the wine from the jar, stir in the last of the sugar and, when it is dissolved, return it to the jar and the excess to the bottle. Leave the wine until fermentation is finished, then siphon the clearing wine off the sediment into a clean jar. Top up from the bottle, add 1 crushed Campden tablet, bung tight, label and store the wine until it is bright.

The wine and sediment left in the jar may be poured into the bottle and left in a cool place until the sediment settles. The clear wine should then be transferred to another bottle and the sediment discarded. The wine can be used for topping up the jar after its racking.

Marigold Wine

Yield: 6 bottles

Classification: Social, medium, white

2.8 L (5 pt) marigold flowers
2 oranges (Seville if possible)
1 lemon
225 g (½ lb) sultanas or raisins
4.5 L (1 gal) water
1 kg (2¼ lb) white sugar
All-purpose wine yeast and nutrient
Campden tablets

Sterilize all equipment as needed and start your records.

Collect the flowers, strip off and discard the leaves, stems and calyx. Put them into a measuring jug and shake them down gently; do not press.

Pare the oranges and lemon, avoiding all white pith. Chop the rind and set it aside. Express and strain the juice, wash and chop the sultanas or raisins.

Put the flower heads into a plastic bin with the orange and lemon rinds and the sultanas or raisins. Pour over the boiling water and leave to cool. Stir in the orange and lemon juice and the activated yeast and nutrient, cover loosely and ferment on the pulp for 5 days, pressing down on the floating fruit and flowers twice daily.

Strain out the solids, pressing until all the juice is extracted. Discard the pulp. Stir in the sugar, then pour the must into a fermentation jar and any excess into a bottle. Fit an airlock to the fermentation jar and plug the neck of the bottle with cotton wool. Leave to ferment out at around 20°C (68°F).

When fermentation is finished, siphon the clearing wine off the sediment into a clean container, add 1 crushed Campden tablet and store until the wine is bright, then bottle.

Keep for 9 months or longer before drinking.

67

Marrow Wine

Yield: 6 to 6½ bottles

Classification: Social, medium, white

2 kg (4½ lb) marrow
1 grapefruit
1 lemon
1 orange
25 g (1 oz) root ginger
225 g (½ lb) sultanas
4.5 L (1 gal) boiling water
All-purpose wine yeast and nutrient
1 kg (2¼ lb) white sugar
Campden tablets

Sterilize all equipment as needed and start your records.

Wipe the marrow and cut it up into dice-sized pieces, using the rind, pulp and seeds – but be careful not to cut the seeds. Place in a polythene bin. Very thinly pare the citrus fruit, excluding all white pith. Express and strain the juice and set aside. Bruise the root ginger well. Wash and chop the sultanas.

Place the fruit parings, ginger and sultanas in the bin with the marrow and pour the water over them. Cover and leave to cool. Add the fruit juice and the activated wine yeast and nutrient. Ferment on the pulp for 5 days, keeping the fruit submerged.

Strain out, press and discard the pulp. Stir in all the sugar. Pour the must into a fermentation jar and any excess into a bottle. Fit an airlock to the jar and a plug of cotton wool to the neck to the bottle. Ferment out until finished.

Siphon the clearing wine off the sediment into clean bottles.

Store for 6 months.

Mint Wine

Yield: 6 bottles

Classification: Social, medium, white

1 L (1¾ pt) fresh mint leaves
2 lemons
450 g (1 lb) sultanas
4.5 L (1 gal) water
All-purpose wine yeast and nutrient
1 kg (2¼ lb) white sugar
Campden tablets

Sterilize all equipment as needed and start your records.

Wash the leaves in running water, chop them up and put them into a boiling pan. Thinly pare the lemon rinds, avoiding all white pith. Express and strain the juice, wash and chop the sultanas.

Bring the water, mint leaves and lemon parings to the boil. Simmer for 10 minutes, then strain into a bin containing the sultanas. Discard the herbs and parings, top up with cold water and, when cool, add the lemon juice and activated wine yeast and nutrient. Cover loosely and ferment for 5 days.

Strain out, press and discard the sultanas. Stir in the sugar. Pour the must into a fermentation jar and any excess into a bottle. Fit an airlock to the jar and a plug of cotton wool into the neck of the bottle. Ferment out at around 18°C (64°F).

Siphon the clearing wine into a clean jar, add 1 crushed Campden tablet, top up with wine from the bottle, bung tight and label.

Store for 3 months before bottling.

Mixed with soda and ice cubes, Mint Wine can make a very refreshing summer drink. Decorate with fresh mint leaves.

Mixed Fruit Wine 1

Yield: 6 to 7 bottles

Classification: Table, dry, rosé

225 g (½ lb) blackcurrants
450 g (1 lb) redcurrants
450 g (1 lb) white currants
225 g (½ lb) raspberries
225 g (½ lb) strawberries
225 g (½ lb) Morello cherries
4.5 L (1 gal) water
5 ml (1 tsp) pectic enzyme
Campden tablets
Bordeaux wine yeast and nutrient
1.35 kg (3 lb) white sugar

Sterilize all equipment as needed and start your records.

Stalk, wash, crush and stone the fruit. Put the crushed fruit, cold water, pectic enzyme and 1 crushed Campden tablet into a suitable container. Cover and leave for 24 hours.

Next day, measure the specific gravity, add the activated wine yeast and nutrient and ferment on the pulp for 3 days, keeping the fruit submerged and the bin loosely covered. Strain out, press dry and discard the fruit, stir in the sugar and fit an airlock.

When fermentation is finished, siphon the wine off its sediment into clean containers. Add 1 crushed Campden tablet and store until the wine is bright, then rack again.

Store the wine in bulk for 9 months, then bottle and store for 3 more. You can sweeten this wine slightly before serving if wished.

Mixed Fruit Wine 2

Yield: 6 to 7 bottles

Classification: Table, dry, white

440 g (15½ oz) can gooseberries
440 g (15½ oz) can golden plums
440 g (15½ oz) can apricots
225 g (½ lb) sultanas
4 L (7 pt) water
5 ml (1 tsp) pectic enzyme
5 ml (1 tsp) citric acid
Campden tablets
All-purpose wine yeast and nutrient
900 g (2 lb) white sugar

Sterilize all equipment as needed and start your records.

Open the cans, strain out and set aside the syrup in a cool place. Wash and chop the sultanas and crush the canned fruit. Put all the fruit into suitable container, cover with cold water, then add the pectic enzyme, citric acid and 1 crushed Campden tablet. Cover the container and leave for 24 hours.

Next day, add the fruit syrup, measure the specific gravity, then add the activated yeast and nutrient. Ferment on the pulp for 3 days, with the fruit submerged and the bin covered.

Strain out and drain the pulp dry without pressing, then discard it. Stir in sugar, pour into a fermentation jar and fit an airlock. Ferment out at a temperature of 18°C (64°F).

When fermentation is finished, siphon the clearing wine off the sediment into a clean container, add 1 Campden tablet, top up with cold boiled water, if necessary, bung tight, label and store. As soon as the wine is bright, siphon it into sterilized bottles, seal and label.

Keep for 3 months before serving.

Variations: The separate ingredients all make excellent wines on their own: use three similar-sized cans of each.

Mixed Herb Wine

Yield: 6 bottles

Classification: Social, medium, white

450 g (1 lb) parsley leaves
50 g (2 oz) mint leaves
50 g (2 oz) mixed other herbs
2 lemons
25 g (1 oz) root ginger
450 g (1 lb) sultanas
4.5 L (1 gal) water
All-purpose wine yeast and nutrient
1 kg (2¼ lb) white sugar
Campden tablets

Sterilize all equipment as needed and start your records.

Remove the parsley and mint leaves from their stalks. Take care not to include any stalks with the leaves. Wash the parsley, mint and other herb leaves in running water, chop them up and put them into a boiling pan. Thinly pare the lemon rinds, avoiding all white pith. Express and strain the juice and set aside. Bruise the root ginger so that the flavour can exude into the liquid. Wash and chop the sultanas.

Bring the water, various herb leaves, lemon parings and bruised root ginger to the boil. Simmer for 10 minutes, then strain into a bin containing the sultanas. Discard the herbs and parings, top up with cold water and, when cool, add the lemon juice and the activated wine yeast and nutrient. Cover loosely and ferment for 5 days.

Strain out, press and discard the sultanas. Stir in the sugar. Pour the must into a fermentation jar and any excess into a bottle. Fit an airlock to the jar and a plug of cotton wool into the neck of the bottle. Ferment out at around 18°C (64°F).

Siphon the clearing wine into a clean jar, add 1 crushed Campden tablet, top up with wine from the bottle, bung tight and label.

Store for 3 months before bottling.

Mulberry 'Madeira'

Yield: 6 bottles

Classification: Dessert, sweet, red

2.7 kg (6 lb) mulberries
225 g (½ lb) raisins
4.5 L (1 gal) water
5 ml (1 tsp) pectic enzyme
Campden tablets
10 ml (2 tsp) citric acid
2.5 ml (½ tsp) grape tannin
Madeira wine yeast and nutrient
1.35 kg (3 lb) Demerara or soft brown sugar

Sterilize all equipment as needed and start your records.

Wash and crush the mulberries. Wash and chop the raisins. Place the prepared mulberries and raisins in the water in a suitable container and heat to 85°C (176°F). Maintain the temperature for 15 minutes. Leave to cool. Strain out the pulp through a fine-meshed nulon bag and press the fruit dry. Discard the pulp. Add the pectic enzyme, 1 crushed Campden tablet and the citric acid. Cover and leave for 24 hours.

Next day, measure the specific gravity. Add the tannin and activated wine yeast and nutrient. Stir in one-third of the brown sugar, pour the must into a fermentation jar and the excess into a bottle. Fit an airlock to the jar and a plug of cotton wool to the bottle and continue the fermentation.

After 1 week, remove half the wine from the jar, stir in half the remaining sugar and return the must slowly to the jar and the excess to the bottle. Repeat the process 1 week later and leave to ferment out.

Siphon the clearing wine into a sterilized jar, add 1 crushed Campden tablet, top up with wine from the bottle, bung tight, label and store. As soon as the wine is bright, rack again.

Store this wine in bulk for at least 1 year and preferably 2. Then bottle and store for a further 6 months. If you wish, you can sweeten the finished wine to your taste when decanting just before serving.

Nettle Wine

Yield: 6 bottles

Classification: Social, medium, green

2.25 L (4 pt) young nettle tops
2 lemons
15 g (½ oz) root ginger
450 g (1 lb) sultanas
4.5 L (1 gal) water
All-purpose wine yeast and nutrient
1 kg (2¼ lb) sugar
Campden tablets

Sterilize all equipment as needed and start your records.

Pick the tops and young leaves of the nettle plant, discarding any coarse stem or withered leaves. Wash them carefully in running water and put them into a boiling pan.

Thinly pare the lemon rinds, avoiding all white pith. Express and strain the juice and set aside. Firmly bruise the root ginger so that the flavour can exude into the liquid. Wash and chop the sultanas.

Bring the water, leaves, lemon parings and bruised root ginger to the boil. Simmer for 45 minutes, then strain into a bin containing the sultanas. Discard the nettles and parings, top up with cold water and, when cool, add the lemon juice and the activated wine yeast and nutrient. Cover loosely and ferment for 5 days.

Strain out, press and discard the sultanas. Stir in the sugar. Pour the must into a fermentation jar and any excess into a bottle. Fit an airlock to the jar and a plug of cotton wool into the neck of the bottle. Ferment out at around 18°C (64°F).

Siphon the clearing wine into a clean jar, add 1 crushed Campden tablet, top up with wine from the bottle, bung tight and label.

Store for 3 months before bottling.

Nettles may seem an unlikely ingredient but a pleasant green, social wine can be made from the nettle tops. Cold tea is another unusual ingredient which produces a distinctive medium white wine (page 86).

Recipes

Oakleaf Wine (instant)

Yield: 6 bottles

Classification: Table, medium, white

4.5 L (1 gal) green oakleaves
4.5 L (1 gal) water
2 lemons
1.13 kg (2½ lb) sugar
5 ml (1 tsp) citric acid
Granulated yeast and nutrient
Campden tablets

Sterilize all equipment as needed and start your records.

Wash the leaves thoroughly and drain them. Boil 3.4 L (6 pt) of water and add 675 g (1½ lb) of sugar; stir well until dissolved. Put the leaves in a polythene bin and pour boiling water over them. Allow it to stand for 24 hours. Express and strain the juice from the lemons; add this juice and the citric acid to the bin and stir well. Strain into a fermentation jar, discard the pulp, then add the yeast and nutrient. Stir well and make up the must to 4.5 L (1 gal). Seal the jar with an airlock and stand it in a warm place, about 21°C (70°F). Maintain this temperature.

After three days, add half of the remaining sugar, dissolved. After a further three days, add the remaining 225 g (½ lb) of sugar, dissolved. If necessary make the must up to 4.5 L (1 gal).

When fermentation has finished, in 14 to 21 days, rack off the wine into a clean jar and add 1 crushed Campden tablet. Allow it to stand for at least seven days, then filter it until clear.

Orange Juice Wine

Yield: 6 bottles

Classification: Aperitif, dry, white

1 L (1¾ pt) carton pure orange juice
3 L (5¼ pt) cold water
900 g (2 lb) white sugar
All-purpose wine yeast and nutrient
Campden tablets

Sterilize all equipment as needed and start your records.

Mix all the ingredients together and, when the sugar is dissolved, pour the must into a fermentation jar. Fit an airlock and ferment out to dryness.

Siphon the clearing wine off the sediment into a clean container. Add 1 crushed Campden tablet and, when bright, bottle, adding 1 saccharin tablet per bottle to take the edge off the dryness.

This wine matures quickly – store for 2–3 months before drinking.

Variations: Other unsweetened fruit juices, notably grapefruit, may be used in the same way.

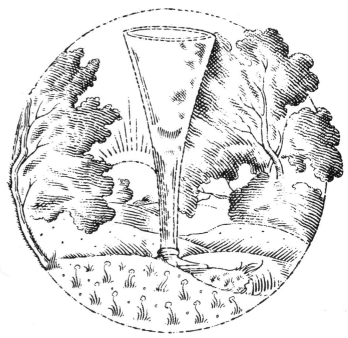

Parsnip Wine

Yield: 6 to 6½ bottles

Classification: Dessert, sweet, golden

2 kg (4½ lb) parsnips
2 lemons
2 oranges
450 g (1 lb) raisins
4.5 L (1 gal) water
Madeira wine yeast and nutrient
1.35 kg (3 lb) light brown sugar
Campden tablets

Sterilize all equipment as needed and start your records.

Use freshly dug parsnips. Scrup them clean and dice small. Thinly pare the lemon and orange rinds, avoiding all white pith. Express and strain the juice and set aside. Wash and chop the raisins.

Place the parsnips in a boiling pan with the lemon and orange rinds. Add enough water comfortably to fill the pan, cover it, bring to the boil and simmer for up to 1½ hours until the parsnips are soft to the fork. Strain the liquor through a nylon strainer or bag into a polythene bin containing the raisins. Top up to the required level, cover the bin and leave the liquor to cool. Then measure the specific gravity and add the lemon and orange juice and activated yeast and nutrient.

Ferment on the raisin pulp for 5 days, keeping the raisins submerged. Strain out, press and discard the raisins. Stir in one-third of the sugar and fit an airlock. Ferment for about 7 days. Remove half the wine, stir in another third of the sugar and return the fermenting must to the jar and the accompanying bottle. About a week later, repeat the process with the last of the sugar and continue the fermentation.

Siphon the clearing wine off the sediment into a clean jar and top up with the wine from the bottle. Add 1 crushed Campden tablet, bung tight, label and store. Pour the residue from the jar into the bottle and, as soon as the sediment settles, pour the clean wine into another bottle that it can just fill.

Mature this wine for 1 year in bulk. Bottle and store for another 1 year before drinking.

Pea Pod Wine (instant)

Yield: 6 bottles

Classification: Table, medium, white

2 kg (4½ lb) young pea pods
4.5 L (1 gal) water
900 g (2 lb) sugar
5 ml (1 tsp) citric acid
2.5 ml (½ tsp) grape tannin
Granulated yeast and nutrient
Campden tablets
5 ml (1 tsp) pectin enzyme

Sterilize all equipment as needed and start your records.

Wash and drain the pea pods. Put them into a pan with a crushed Campden tablet. Add 4.5 L (1 gal) of water and boil this until the pods are tender. Strain the juice liquor into a fermentation jar and discard the pulp. Dissolve all the sugar in warm water and add this to the jar, together with the citric acid, tannin and pectin enzyme. Stir thoroughly and after 24 hours add the yeast and nutrient. Seal the jar with an airlock.

Stand the jar in a warm place, about 21°C (70°F), maintaining this temperature. When fermentation has finished, in 14 to 21 days, rack off the wine into a clean jar and add 1 crushed Campden tablet. Allow the wine to stand for at least seven days, then filter it until clear and bottle. This wine will not keep, consume it within two weeks.

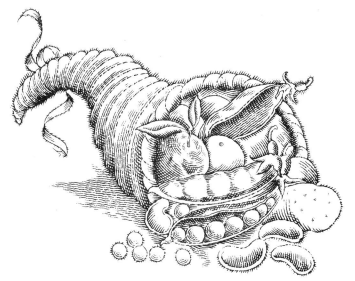

Peach Wine

Yield: 6 to 7 bottles

Classification: Table, sweet, white

2 kg (4½ lb) ripe peaches
250 g (9 oz) sultanas
3.4 L (6 pt) water
15 g (½ oz) citric acid
5 ml (1 tsp) pectic enzyme
Sauternes wine yeast and nutrient
1 kg (2¼ lb) white sugar
Campden tablets

Sterilize all equipment as needed and start your records.

Peel, stone and crush the peaches; wash and chop the sultanas. Put the fruit into a bin containing the water, citric acid, pectic enzyme and 1 crushed Campden tablet. Cover and leave for 24 hours. Add the activated yeast and nutrient and ferment on the pulp for 4 days, keeping the fruit submerged.

Strain out, press dry and discard the pulp. Stir in the sugar and, when it is dissolved, pour the must into a fermentation jar and any excess into a bottle. Fit an airlock to the jar and a plug of cotton wool to the neck of the bottle. Ferment out at around 18°C (64°F).

From time to time, check the specific gravity of the liquid and, when 1.016 is reached, rack the wine into a sterilized jar containing 1 g of potassium sorbate and 1 crushed Campden tablet. Seal the jar and store in a cool place.

When the wine is bright, rack again and store for 6 months before bottling. Keep for a further 3 months at least before serving, nicely chilled.

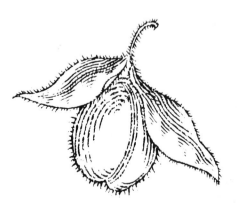

Plum Wine

Yield: 6 bottles

Classification: Aperitif, sweet, red

2 kg (4½ lb) Victoria plums
225 g (½ lb) sultanas
4.5 L (1 gal) boiling water
5 ml (1 tsp) pectic enzyme
10 ml (2 tsp) citric acid
Campden tablets
Sherry wine yeast and nutrient
1.35 kg (3 lb) white sugar

Sterilize all equipment as needed and start your records.

Wash, stone and crush the fruit. Wash and chop the sultanas. Put the crushed fruit into a bin with the sultanas and pour over the water. Cover and leave it to cool. Add the pectic enzyme, citric acid and 1 crushed Campden tablet to the bin and then leave for 24 hours.

Add the activated yeast and nutrient and ferment on the pulp for 5 days, keeping the pulp submerged and the bin loosely covered.

Strain out, press dry and then discard the pulp. Stir in one-third of the sugar, cover loosely to allow the gas to escape, and continue fermentation in the bin for a further 1 week. Stir in half the remaining sugar and ferment as before for 1 week, then stir in the remaining sugar, and ferment.

Measure the specific gravity with a hydrometer and, when the reading is very low, say 1.002, add a further 225 g (½ lb) of sugar if the fermentation is still proceeding. Try to finish the wine dry or nearly so.

Siphon the new wine off the sediment and add a crushed Campden tablet. Plug with cotton wool and leave to mature in containers not quite full.

Keep for at least 1 year before drinking, preferably longer.

Victoria plums make a strong sherry-type wine, whilst the red and black varieties, surprisingly, make rosé wines because the skins lack colour. Golden plums and greengages can be used to make white table wines.

Potato Wine

Yield: 6 to 6½ bottles

Classification: Social, sweet, white

2 kg (4½ lb) potatoes
2 lemons
2 oranges
15 g (½ oz) root ginger
4.5 L (1 gal) water
450 g (1 lb) raisins
Madeira wine yeast and nutrient
1.35 kg (3 lb) light brown sugar
Campden tablets

Sterilize all equipment as needed and start your records.

Use main crop potatoes if at all possible – new potatoes are not suitable. Scrub them well and cut into small dice-sized pieces. Thinly pare the lemons and oranges (Seville if available), avoiding all white pith. Express and strain the juice and set aside. Bruise the ginger.

Boil the potatoes, fruit parings, ginger and water together for 30 minutes – no longer. Strain the liquor onto the washed and chopped raisins in a polythene bin. Top up to the required level, cover the bin and leave the liquor to cool. Then measure the specific gravity and add the lemon and orange juice and activated yeast and nutrient.

Ferment on the raisin pulp for 5 days, keeping the raisins submerged. Strain out, press and discard the raisins. Stir in one-third of the sugar and fit an airlock. Ferment for about 7 days. Remove half the wine, stir in another third of the sugar and return the fermenting must to the jar and the accompanying bottle. About a week later, repeat the process with the last of the sugar and continue the fermentation.

Siphon the clearing wine off the sediment into a clean jar and top up with the wine from the bottle. Add 1 crushed Campden tablet, bung tight, label and store. Pour the residue from the jar into the bottle, and, as soon as the sediment settles, pour the clean wine into another bottle that it can just fill.

Mature this wine for 1 year in bulk. Bottle and store for another 1 year before drinking.

Prune Wine

Yield: 6 bottles

Classification: Aperitif, medium, red

900 g (2 lb) prunes
4 L (7 pt) water
900 g (2 lb) raisins
10 ml (2 tsp) citric acid
Sherry wine yeast and nutrient
1 kg (2¼ lb) soft brown sugar
Campden tablets

Sterilize all equipment as needed and start your records.

Wash the prunes and soak them overnight in hot water. Next day, remove the stones and wash and chop up the raisins.

Add the raisins, citric acid and activated sherry wine yeast and nutrient to the prunes and liquid in which they were soaked. Cover loosely to allow the gas to escape and ferment on the pulp for 7 days, keeping the fruit submerged.

Strain out, press the fruit dry and discard the pulp. Measure the specific gravity. Stir in one-third of the sugar, cover loosely to allow more gas to escape and continue fermentation in the bin for a further 1 week. Stir in half the remaining sugar and ferment as before for 1 week, then stir in the remaining sugar, and ferment.

Measure the specific gravity with a hydrometer and, when the reading is very low, say 1.002, add a further 225 g (½ lb) of sugar if the fermentation is still proceeding. Try to finish the wine dry or nearly so.

Siphon the new wine off the sediment and add a crushed Campden tablet. Plug with cotton wool and leave to mature in containers not quite full.

Keep for at least 1 year before drinking, preferably longer.

Recipes

Rhubarb Wine

Yield: 6 to 7 bottles

Classification: Table, medium, rosé

2.7 kg (6 lb) rhubarb stalks
1 orange
1.35 kg (3 lb) white sugar
4.5 L (1 gal) water
All-purpose wine yeast and nutrient
Campden tablets

Cut off the rhubarb leaves together with 2.5 cm (1 in) top and bottom of the stalks. (This ensure that the stalks contains no unpleasant constituent such as oxalic acid.) Wipe each stalk with a clean cloth dipped in a sulphite solution made from half a Campden tablet and a pinch of citric acid dissolved in an additional cup of cold water. This removes most of the invisible moulds, fungi and bacteria as well as dust and soil.

Sterilize all equipment as needed and start your records. Crush, chop or mince the rhubarb stalks and place them in a polythene bin together with the wiped, thinly pared and chopped up rind of the orange, devoid of all white pith. Cut the orange in half, express and strain the juice and set aside.

Place the orange rind and juice and one-third of the sugar in the bin containing the rhubarb. Pour on the cold water and stir well until the sugar is dissolved. Add the activated yeast and nutrient. Ferment on the pulp for 5 days. Keep the fruit submerged or press it down twice daily.

Strain out and press the fruit dry, discarding the pulp. Stir in the rest of the sugar and pour the must into a sterilized fermentation jar and the excess into a bottle. Fit an airlock to the jar and plug the neck of the bottle with cotton wool. Ferment out at a steady temperature of around 17°C (62°F), or just a little lower.

When fermentation is finished, move the wine to a cold place for a few days, then siphon it off its sediment into a sterilized jar. Add a crushed Campden tablet, top up with wine from the bottle, label and store until the wine is bright. The small amount of wine left in the fermentation jar may be poured into the wine remaining in the bottle and, when the sediment has settled, the clear wine should be transferred to a bottle of a size that it will just fill.

Keep this wine for 1 year before drinking it.

Note: The body and vinosity of this wine can be improved by adding 225 g (½ lb) of washed and chopped sultanas to the rhubarb.

Rice Wine

Yield: 6 bottles

Classification: Social, sweet, golden

1.35 kg (3 lb) crushed brown rice
2 lemons
450 g (1 lb) raisins
4.5 L (1 gal) boiling water
Cereal wine yeast and nutrient
1.35 kg (3 lb) white or light brown sugar
Campden tablets

Sterilize all equipment as needed and start your records.

If the rice is not already crushed, grind it coarsely in a mincing machine. Alternatively, soak it in a little hot water for an hour to soften it a little. Drain off the surplus water, place the grains on a hard smooth surface and roll them with a ceramic or hard-wood roller to crack grains. (Polished rice is not so suitable. Flaked rice could be used, but much of the goodness has gone.)

Thinly pare the lemon rinds, avoiding all white pith. Express and strain the juice. Wash and chop the raisins. Place the rice in a bin with the lemon rind and raisins. Pour over the boiling water and leave to cool.

Add the activated cereal wine yeast and nutrient and the lemon juice. Cover loosely and ferment on the pulp for 7 days, keeping the pulp submerged.

Strain out, press and discard the pulp. Stir in one-third of the sugar. Pour the must into a fermentation jar and any excess into a bottle. Fit an airlock to the jar and plug the neck of the bottle with cotton wool. Ferment for 1 week.

Remove half the wine from the jar and stir in another third of the sugar. After a further week, again remove half the wine from the jar, stir in the last of the sugar and, when it is dissolved, return it to the jar and the excess to the bottle. Leave the wine until fermentation is finished, then siphon the clearing wine off the sediment into a clean jar. Top up from the bottle, add 1 crushed Campden tablet, bung tight, label and then store the wine until it is completely bright.

The wine and sediment left in the jar may be poured into the bottle and left in a cool place until the sediment settles. The clear wine should then be transferred to another bottle and the sediment discarded. The wine can be used for topping up the jar after its racking.

Store in bulk for at least 2 years, then bottle and keep for a further year or more. It does not really begin to be enjoyable until it is at least 3 years old but by then it is very smooth indeed.

Rosehip and Fig Wine

Yield: 6 bottles

Classification: Aperitif, sweet, red

2.3 L (4 pt) fresh rosehips or
225 g (½ lb) dried rosehip shells
225 g (½ lb) raisins
1 lemon
115 g (¼ lb) dried figs
4 L (7 pt) water
5 ml (1 tsp) pectic enzyme
15 ml (3 tsp) citric acid
Sherry wine yeast and nutrient
1.35 kg (3 lb) Demerara or light brown sugar
Campden tablets

Sterilize all equipment as needed and start your records.

Trim the fresh rosehips, rinse them in clean cold water and crush them. Wash and chop the raisins. Thinly pare the lemon rind, avoiding all white pith, express and strain the juice and set aside.

Place the crushed rosehips, lemon rind, figs (broken into small pieces) and water in a suitable container and heat to 80°C (176°F). Maintain the temperature for 15 minutes. Cover the pan and leave to cool. Strain the liquor onto the raisins and press and discard the pulp. Add the expressed and strained lemon juice, the pectic enzyme, citric acid and the activated sherry yeast and nutrient. Ferment on the raisin pulp for 5 days, keeping them submerged.

Strain out, press dry and discard the raisins. Stir in one-third of the sugar and continue the fermentation in the bin, loosely covered. Stir in the rest of the sugar in two equal doses at weekly intervals and leave to ferment out.

When fermentation is finished, siphon the clearing wine off its sediment into a sterilized storage jar and a large bottle, leaving a good headspace in both. Plug both containers with cotton wool and mature for 18 months, racking when a sediment is thrown and the wine is bright. Bottle, seal and label.

Rosehips, ideally gathered from the hedgerows, mixed with dried figs make a sweet, red wine which is rich in vitamins and minerals.

Rose Petal Wine

Yield: 6 to 6½ bottles

Classification: Social, medium, white

2.25 L (½ gal) rose petals
1 orange
2 lemons
225 g (½ lb) sultanas
4.5 L (1 gal) boiling water
All-purpose wine yeast and nutrient
1 kg (2¼ lb) sugar
Campden tablets

Sterilize all equipment as needed and start your records.

To measure the rose petals, put them into a measuring jug and shake them down gently; do not press. Pare the orange and lemons, avoiding all white pith, then chop the rind and set it aside. Express and strain the juice, wash and chop the sultanas.

Put the rose petals into a plastic bin with the orange and lemon rinds and the sultanas. Pour over the boiling water, cover and leave to cool. Add the fruit juice and yeast and nutrient, cover loosely and leave to ferment for 5 days, pressing down the floating petals and fruit twice daily.

Strain the must through a nylon mesh bag into a container, pressing until all the juice is extracted. Stir in the sugar. Pour the liquid into a fermentation jar and any excess into a bottle. Fit an airlock into the fermentation jar and plug the neck of the bottle with cotton wool. Leave to ferment out at a temperature of about 20°C (68°F).

When fermentation is finished, move the wine to a cool place for a few days to help it to clear. Siphon the clearing wine off the sediment into a clean jar. Add 1 crushed Campden tablet and top up the jar (if necessary) with wine from the bottle. Bung tight, label and store in a cool place until bright and clear.

Rack again, then mature in bulk for 6 months before bottling. Keep for 1 year before drinking, and sweeten to taste before serving.

Scotch Broom or Gorse Wine

Yield: 6 bottles

Classification: Social, medium, golden

4.5 L (1 gal) fresh gorse flowers
1 orange
2 lemons
225 g (½ lb) sultanas
4.5 L (1 gal) boiling water
All-purpose wine yeast and nutrient
1 kg (2¼ lb) sugar
Campden tablets

Sterilize all equipment as needed and start your records.

To measure the gorse flowers, put them into a measuring jug and shake them down gently; do not press. Pare the orange and lemons, avoiding all white pith, then chop the rind and set it aside. Express and strain the juice, wash and chop the sultanas.

Put the blooms into a plastic bin with the orange and lemon rinds, and the sultanas. Pour over the boiling water and leave to cool. Stir in the orange and lemon juice, activated yeast and nutrient, cover loosely and leave to ferment for 5 days, pressing down the floating flowers and fruit twice daily.

Strain the must through a nylon mesh bag into a container, pressing until all the juice is extracted. Stir in the sugar. Pour the liquid into a fermentation jar and any excess into a bottle. Fit an airlock into the fermentation jar and plug the neck of the bottle with cotton wool. Leave to ferment out at a temperature of about 20°C (68°F).

When fermentation is finished, move the wine to a cool place for a few days to help it to clear. Siphon the clearing wine off the sediment into a clean jar. Add 1 crushed Campden tablet and top up the jar (if necessary) with wine from the bottle. Bung tight, label and store in a cool place until bright and clear.

Rack again, then mature in bulk for 6 months before bottling. Keep for 1 year before drinking, and sweeten to taste before serving.

Fresh Scotch broom or gorse flowers, gathered in the mid-spring, can make a medium, golden wine for drinking on all occasions.

Sherry Wine

Yield: 6 bottles

Classification: Aperitif, medium, red

1 can, 1 kg (2¼ lb) sherry grape juice concentrate
Water
Sherry-type yeast and nutrient
Campden tablets
85 ml (3 fl oz) vodka, 100° proof

Sterilize all equipment as needed and start your records.

Pour the concentrate into a jug, rinsing out any juice from the can with very hot water. Pour the contents of the jug into the fermentation jar, then add warm water to make up to 3.4 L (6 pt).

Dissolve half of the sugar in warm water and add this to the jar; stir well, then add the yeast and yeast nutrient, and seal the jar with an airlock.

Stand the jar in a warm place, about 21°C (70°F), maintaining this temperature. After three days, add half of the remaining sugar, dissolved. After a further three days, add the remaining 57 g (2 oz) of sugar, dissolved, and make the total quantity of must up to 4.5 L (1 gal) with warm water.

Fermentation should finish in 14 to 21 days from commencement; when finished, rack off the wine. Stand the wine for one week, then filter it repeatedly.

When the wine is matured it will have a sherry flavour, but real sherry is fortified. If you like what you have made, put 85 ml (3 fl oz) of 100° proof vodka into a wine bottle and fill it with the sherry. Seal the bottle and leave if for a few days before use.

Strawberry Wine

Yield: 6 bottles

Classification: Table, medium, rosé

1.8 kg (4 lb) ripe strawberries
1.35 kg (3 lb) sugar
4.5 L (1 gal) water
10 ml (2 tsp) citric acid
2.5 ml (½ tsp) grape tannin
All-purpose yeast and nutrient
Campden tablets
5 ml (1 tsp) pectin enzyme

Sterilize all equipment as needed and start your records.

Hull the strawberries, wash them well and allow them to drain. Dissolve the sugar in a little hot water, add the strawberries and mash them thoroughly. Add 2.3 L (½ gal) of warm water and leave in a covered polythene bin for two days. Add the citric acid, tannin and pectin destroying enzyme. Stand for 24 hours.

Add a further 2.3 L (½ gal) of warm water, stir well and strain into the fermentation jar and discard the pulp. Add the yeast and nutrient, and seal the jar with an airlock.

When fermentation is complete, strain the must into a clean jar, add one crushed Campden tablet and close the container with a bung or safety lock. Rack after two months and again before bottling. Ideally, leave for 1–2 years to mature.

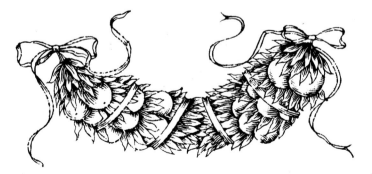

Wine made from strawberries is a lovely rosé colour and can look very attractive on a table. It is medium-sweet in flavour and is suitable for drinking with meals.

Tea Wine

Yield: 6 bottles

Classification: Social, medium, white

4.5 L (1 gal) strong cold tea
2 lemons
450 g (1 lb) raisins
All-purpose wine yeast and nutrient
1 kg (2¼ lb) sugar
Campden tablets

Sterilize all equipment as needed and start your records.

Collect the tea left over from the pot after each brew until you have a gallon. Alternatively, pour 4.5 L (1 gal) of boiling water onto 16 tea bags and leave covered until it is cool. Remove, press and discard the bags.

Thinly pare and chop the lemon rinds, avoiding all white pith. Express and strain the juice. Wash and chop the raisins.

Put the cold tea, the lemon rinds and juice, raisins and activated yeast and nutrient into a plastic bin. Ferment for 5 days, keeping the raisins submerged. Strain out, press and discard the raisins and rind. Stir in the sugar.

Pour the must into a fermentation jar and any excess into a bottle. Fit an airlock to the jar and a plug of cotton wool into the neck of the bottle. Ferment out at around 18°C (64°F).

Siphon the clearing wine into a clean jar, add 1 crushed Campden tablet, top up with wine from the bottle, bung tight and label.

Store for 3 months before bottling.

Tree Leaf Wine

Yield: 6 bottles

Classification: Social, medium, white

3.35 L (6 pt) oak leaves or
550 ml (1 pt) walnut leaves
2 lemons
4.5 L (1 gal) water
450 g (1 lb) sultanas or raisins
All-purpose wine yeast and nutrient
1 kg (2¼ lb) white sugar
Campden tablets

Sterilize all equipment as needed and start your records.

Wash the young oak or walnut leaves in running water and shake them dry in a salad basket or colander. Chop them up lightly and put them into a measuring jug, shaking them down gently; do not press. Thinly pare the lemon rinds, avoiding all white pith. Express and strain the juice and set aside. Wash and chop the sultanas or raisins.

Bring the water, oak or walnut leaves and lemon parings to the boil. Simmer for 10 minutes, then strain into a bin containing the sultanas. Discard the leaves and parings, top up with cold water and, when cool, add the lemon juice and the activated wine yeast and nutrient. Cover loosely and ferment for 5 days.

Strain out, press and discard the sultanas. Stir in the sugar. Pour the must into a fermentation jar and any excess into a bottle. Fit an airlock to the jar and a plug of cotton wool into the neck of the bottle. Ferment out at around 18°C (64°F).

Siphon the clearing wine into a clean jar, add 1 crushed Campden tablet, top up with wine from the bottle, bung tight and label. Store for 3 months before bottling.

Note: These leaves contribute only tannin and a little flavour. It is essential to include the lemons to provide acid and the sultanas or raisins to provide some body and vinosity. An equal quantity of honey may be subsituted for up to half the sugar, if desired.

Vermouth Wine

Yield: 6 bottles

Classification: Aperitif, medium, white or red

1 can, 1 kg (2¼ lb) Vermouth grape concentrate
Water
Sugar as called for on can
All-purpose or Vermouth-type yeast and nutrient
Campden tablets

Sterilize all equipment as needed and start your records.

Pour the concentrate into a jug, rinsing out any juice from the can with very hot water. Pour the contents of the jug into the fermentation jar, then add warm water to make up to 3.4 L (6 pt).

Dissolve half of the sugar in warm water and add this to the jar; stir well, then add the yeast and nutrient, and seal the jar with an airlock.

Stand the jar in a warm place, about 21°C (70°F), maintaining this temperature. After three days, add half of the remaining sugar, dissolved. After a further three days, add the remaining 57 g (2 oz) of sugar, dissolved, and make the total quantity of must up to 4.5 L (1 gal) with warm water.

Fermentation should finish in 14 to 21 days from commencement; when finished, rack off the wine into a clean jar and add 1 crushed Campden tablet. Stand the wine for one week, then filter it repeatedly until clear and then bottle. This wine can be drunk within two weeks of clearing.

Variations: Real vermouth is a fortified wine. The above wine will have a vermouth flavour and can be drunk as it is or fortified by the addition of 85 ml (3 fl oz) of 100° proof vodka per bottle. But make sure that you like the wine before adding the spirit.

Vin Ordinaire (instant)

Yield: 6 bottles

Classification: Table, medium, red, white or rosé

1 can, 1 kg (2¼ lb) of red, white or rosé
grape juice concentrate
Water
225 g (½ lb) sugar
Granulated yeast and nutrient
Campden tablets

Sterilize all equipment as needed and start your records.

Pour the concentrate into a jug, rinsing out any juice from the can with very hot water. Pour the contents of the jug into the fermentation jar, then add warm water to make up to 3.4 L (6 pt).

Dissolve half of the sugar in warm water and add this to the jar; stir well, then add the yeast and nutrient, and seal the jar with an airlock.

Stand the jar in a warm place, about 21°C (70°F), maintaining this temperature. After three days, add half of the remaining sugar, dissolved. After a further three days, add the remaining 57 g (2 oz) of sugar, dissolved, and make the total quantity of must up to 4.5 L (1 gal) with warm water.

Fermentation should finish in 14 to 21 days from commencement; when finished, rack off the wine into a clean jar and add 1 crushed Campden tablet. Stand the wine for one week, then filter it repeatedly until clear and then bottle. This wine can be drunk within two weeks of clearing.

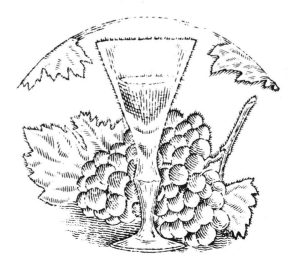

Wheat Wine

Yield: 6 bottles

Classification: Dessert, sweet, golden

900 g (2 lb) crushed wheat
2 lemons
2 sweet oranges
450g (1 lb) raisins
4.5 L (1 gal) boiling water
Cereal wine yeast and nutrient
1.35 kg (3 lb) Demerara sugar
Campden tablets

Sterilize all equipment as needed and start your records.

Thinly pare the lemons and oranges avoiding all white pith, and express and strain the juice. Wash and chop the raisins.

Put the wheat into a bin with the lemon and orange rind and raisins. Pour over the boiling water, cover and leave to cool.

Add the cereal wine yeast and nutrient and lemon and orange juice to the bin and stir well. Cover loosely and ferment on the pulp for 7 days, keeping the pulp submerged. Strain out, press and discard the pulp. Stir in one-third of the sugar. Pour the must into a fermentation jar and any excess into a bottle. Fit an airlock to the jar and plug the neck of the bottle with cotton wool. Ferment for 1 week.

Remove half the wine from the jar and stir in another third of the sugar. After a further week, again remove half the wine from the jar, stir in the last of the sugar and, when it is dissolved, return it to the jar and the excess to the bottle. Leave the wine until fermentation is finished, then siphon the clearing wine off the sediment into a clean jar. Top up from the bottle, add 1 crushed Campden tablet, bung tight, label and store the wine until it is bright.

The wine and sediment left in the jar may be poured into the bottle and left in a cool place until the sediment settles. The clear wine should then be transferred to another bottle and the sediment discarded. This wine can be used for topping up the jar after its racking.

Store in bulk for at least 1 year, then bottle and keep for a further year.

The distinctive sweet flavours of Wheat, Rice (page 79) and Ginger Wine (page 63) are all suitable for blending with thinner, more acidic wines.

White Currant Wine

Yield: 6 bottles

Classification: Table, dry, white

1.35 kg (3 lb) white currants
225g (½ lb) sultanas
4 L (7 pt) water
5 ml (1 tsp) pectic enzyme
Campden tablets
Chablis wine yeast and nutrient
900 g (2 lb) white sugar

Sterilize all equipment as needed and start your records.

Stalk, wash and crush the currants. Wash and chop the sultanas. Add the prepared fruit to the cold water, pectic enzyme and 1 crushed Campden tablet. Cover and leave for 24 hours.

Next day, measure the specific gravity. Add the activated yeast and nutrient and ferment on the pulp for 4 days, keeping the fruit submerged. Strain out, press and discard the fruit. Stir in the sugar and fit an airlock. Ferment out at around 16°C (61°F).

When fermentation is complete, siphon the wine into a clean storage container. Add 1 crushed Campden tablet.

Mature for 6 months before bottling as a table wine, or re-ferment as a sparkling wine by following the instructions given on page 35.

White Wine Cup

Yield: 10 glasses

Classification: Social, sweet, white

1 lemon
3 sugar cubes
12 crushed ice cubes
115 ml (4 fl oz) gin, vodka or white rum
1 bottle sweet white wine, such as peach
6 thin slices unpeeled cucumber
550 ml (1 pt) soda water

Rub the zest off the lemon and add to the sugar, then express and strain the juice.

Put the crushed ice cubes, sugar cubes, lemon juice, gin and wine into a suitable bowl. Stir all the ingredients gently to dissolve the sugar, float the cucumber slices on the top for decoration and then add the mineral water.

Serve immediately. This cup is ideal for a warm summer's day.

White Currant Wine is a good dry white table wine which will be at its best when served properly chilled.

Chapter 4
Liqueur and Brandy Recipes

Very acceptable coloured liqueurs or fruit brandies can be made by steeping fruit like raspberries, oranges, sloes or blackcurrants and sugar in colourless spirits – vodka, eau de vie, white rum and gin are ideal. The amount of fruit you need to use varies with how strong a flavour you want to achieve, but normally 450 g (1 lb) of fruit to a standard bottle of spirit is sufficient. The liqueurs and brandies should be stored from as little as a few weeks to up to a year, and an alcholic strength of 20–35% can be achieved.

Advocaat

Yield: 1 bottle

300 ml (½ pt) water
115 g (¼ lb) white sugar
1 vanilla pod
6 egg yokes
½ standard bottle vodka

Sterilize all equipment as needed and start your records.

Bring the water, sugar and vanilla pod to the boil and stir until the sugar is dissolved. Remove the vanilla pod. Separate the eggs. Beat the egg yolks thoroughly, and *very slowly* add the hot syrup, beating the eggs vigorously so that they do not curdle. This must be done carefully; if the egg yolks boil, they will scramble, with disastrous results! Stir in the vodka and bottle at once.

Seal and label and keep in a cool dark place. Store for 1 week before serving.

Variations: Other recipes include the zest of a lemon rind instead of vanilla, 150 g (5 oz) instead of 115 g (¼ lb) sugar; rum or brandy instead of vodka; and so on. Others replace half the water with fresh single cream or evaporated unsweetened milk to make an even richer drink.

Blackcurrant Rum

Yield: 1⅓ bottles

225 g (½ lb) blackcurrants
225 g (½ lb) caster sugar
1 standard bottle white rum

Sterilize all equipment as needed and start your records.

Stalk, wash and mash the blackcurrants. Place the fruit and sugar in a jar or crock, pour on the rum and stir until the sugar is dissolved. Seal and leave for 1 week, gently shaking the jar daily.

Strain out, drain and gently press the fruit, pour the rum into suitable bottles, seal and label. Store for 1 year before drinking.

Coffee Rum

Yield: 2.25 L (1 qt)

300 ml (½ pt) strong black coffee
300 g (10 oz) soft brown sugar
1 standard bottle vodka

Sterilize all equipment as needed and start your records.

Use the best quality, freshly ground coffee that you can obtain. Place 15 ml (1 tsp) in a jug, pour on 300 ml (½ pt) of hot water and leave for 5 minutes. Place the sugar in a suitable container and pour the coffee through a fine nylon strainer on to it. Stir gently until the sugar is dissolved. Cover and leave to cool. Mix in the vodka and pour into suitable bottles, seal and label. Keep for 1 year before serving.

Advocaat is a rich, creamy liqueur which should be made with care so that the egg yolks do not curdle. Serve it in classic port wine glasses.

Fruit Brandy

Yield: 1 L (1¾ pt)

450 g (1 lb) fruit
175–225 g (6–9 oz) caster sugar
1 standard bottle eau de vie or vodka
15 ml (½ fl oz) glycerine
12 drops capsicum tincture (if available)

Sterilize all equipment as needed and start your records.

Clean, peel, stone and cut up the fruit as required. Place the prepared fruit in a jar or crock in layers, covering each layer with caster sugar. (The precise amount of sugar used will depend on the ripeness and sweetness of the fruit and your own palate – ripe apricots and peaches clearly need less than raspberries and loganberries.) Pour on the spirits, seal the jar and shake it gently to help dissolve the sugar and diffuse the juice.

Store the labelled jar in a cool dark place for 3 months, giving it an occasional shake to distribute the fruit flavour.

After 3 months, strain off the fruit brandy into suitable bottles, seal, label and store for another month before serving.

Orange Gin

Yield: 1⅛ bottles

Metric/Imperial
1 Seville orange
1 sweet orange
225 g (½ lb) sugar
1 standard bottle gin

Sterilize all equipment as needed and start your records.

Very thinly pare the orange rinds, avoiding all white pith, and chop finely. Express and strain the juice. Place the orange rind and juice in a jar or crock and add the sugar. Pour on the gin, stirring gently until all the sugar is dissolved and the spirit is clear. Seal and store in a cool dark place for 1 week, shaking it gently each day.

Strain through a fine nylon strainer into suitable bottles, seal and label. Store for 1 year before drinking.

Large kilner-type jars are the most suitable containers in which to prepare fruit brandies. The fruit should be added in layers with the sugar, and then steeped in the alcohol which is being used.

Raspberry Gin

Yield: 2 full bottles

300 g (10 oz) ripe raspberries
1 standard bottle gin
550 ml (1 pt) hot water
300 g (10 oz) white sugar

Sterilize all equipment as needed and start your records.

Wash the raspberries and either leave whole or cut in half. Place the raspberries in a jar or crock, pour on the gin, seal and leave in a warm place for 1 week, shaking it every day. Dissolve the sugar in hot water until it is transparent then leave it to cool.

Pour the raspberry gin through a fine strainer on to the cool syrup and stir well. Bottle, seal and label. Store for a few weeks so that the spirit and syrup can homogenize.

Sloe Gin

Yield: 1 ⅛ bottles

350 g (12 oz) selected sloes
175 g (6 oz) caster sugar
1 standard bottle gin

Sterilize all equipment as needed and start your records.

Use the largest and blackest sloes you can find. Stalk, wash and prick them all over. Place the sloes in a jar in layers, covering each layer with sugar. Pour on the gin. Leave for 3 months, shaking occasionally to distribute the flavour.

Strain out and discard the sloes. Bottle, seal and label, Store for 1 year to mature.

Variations: If you use a sweet gin, the amount of sugar in the recipe can be reduced. If the final result is not as sweet as you would like, the gin may be sweetened before serving.

Raspberry Gin with its attractive red colour can look superb when stored in a decanter.

Glossary of Terms Used

Acid
The sharp taste of fruits and liquids due to the presence of citric, malic or tartaric acid.

Airlock
A device used to exclude air while permitting gas formed during fermentation to escape.

Alcohol
In the context of this book the word alcohol refers to ethyl alcohol, the spirit that is present in beer, cider, mead and wine and that is added to liqueurs of all kinds.

Campden tablet
The proprietary name for 0.44 g of compressed sodium metabisulphite. One tablet dissolved in one 4.5 L (1 gal) of a liquid releases 50 parts per million of sulphur dioxide. See also *SULPHITE*.

Carbon dioxide
The gas that is given off during the fermentation of sugars into wines.

Dry
A beverage in which there is a lack of sweetness. The opposite of sweet.

Enzyme
A substance which acts as a catalyst in specific circumstances. Each enzyme can cause, by its very presence, a single change in substance, without being changed itself. The name of an enzyme always ends with the letters 'ase', e.g. diastase, maltase, sucrase, zymase.

Fermentation
The process in which yeast converts the sugar in a liquid to alcohol and carbon dioxide.

Ferment on
Continue the fermentation after the removal of pulp or the addition of sugar.

Fermentation-on-the-pulp
Fermentation in the presence of crushed fruit, etc. to extract colour and soluble ingredients.

Ferment out
Continue the fermentation until all the sugar has been converted to alcohol and carbon dioxide.

Hydrometer
An instrument that, in the context of this book, measures the weight of sugar in a liquid.

Invert sugar The name given to a mixture of fructose and glucose after they have been separated in ordinary household sugar.

Maturation The ageing of a wine to the point at which it is most pleasant to drink.

Must The name given to a liquid, with or without solids, before it is fermented into wine.

Nutrient Salts of ammonia added to provide nitrogen for the yeast, e.g. ammonium sulphate and/or diammonium phosphate. Sometimes a few milligrames of vitamin B1 are also added.

Pectic enzyme An enzyme in powder or liquid form which is added to a fruit must to break down the pectin in the fruit. It improves juice extraction and prevents pectic haze in the finished wine.

Rack The process of removing a wine from a sediment which is formed during fermentation or maturation. Usually performed with the aid of a siphon.

Sediment The dross of insoluble particles and yeast cells that collect in the bottom of a container of fermented wine. It can be pasty, flocculent or sandy.

Siphon A length of hose used to transfer a liquid from one vessel to another without disturbing the sediment.

Specific gravity The weight of a given volume of a liquid compared with same volume of water at a temperature of 15°C/59°F.

Starter bottle A bottle containing water, fruit, acid, sugar and nutrient in which dormant yeast cells are reactivated.

Sulphite The abbreviated name of sodium or potassium metabisulphite. Used in solution, often with citric acid, to sterilize equipment and ingredients and to prevent oxidation.

Tannin A bitter substance found in grape stalks, pips and skins that gives character and firmness to a wine.

Yeast Microscopic botanical cells that cause fermentation. The yeasts referred to in this book are called *Saccharomyces* – meaning sugar fungi. There are numerous strains of the major sub-variety *Saccharomyces cerevisiae elipsoideus* (wine yeast).

Sugar and Alcohol Content Tables

Specific Gravity	In 4.50 litres g	Probable percentage alcohol after fermentation
1.005	78	
1.010	134	0.4
1.015	198	1.2
1.020	255	2.0
1.025	311	2.8
1.030	375	3.6
1.035	438	4.3
1.040	496	5.1
1.045	553	5.8
1.050	608	6.5
1.055	672	7.2
1.060	729	7.9
1.065	785	8.6
1.070	849	9.3
1.075	908	10.0
1.080	979	10.6
1.085	1035	11.3
1.090	1092	12.0
1.095	1153	12.7
1.100	1210	13.4
1.105	1266	14.2
1.110	1330	14.9
1.115	1387	15.6
1.120	1450	16.3
1.125	1507	17.1
1.130	1570	17.8

Note: 1 kg sugar occupies 620 ml of volume
2 lb sugar occupies 1 pint of volume
Specific gravity figures are for liquids at 15°C/59°F
   at 20°C/68°F add 1 to the last figure
   at 25°C/77°F add 2
   at 30°C/86°F add 3½
   at 35°C/95°F add 5

Note: Metric and Imperial conversions are *not* exact.
Use one or the other when making the recipes – never mix them.

Useful Weights and Temperatures

	°C	°F
Freezing	0	32
Serve sparkling wine and cold cups	6	43
Serve white and rosé wines	9	48
Serve sherry-type wines	10	50
Ferment white wines	15	59
Ferment red and all strong wines	20	68
Serve red wines and liqueurs		
Prepare yeast starter bottle	23.5	74
Fermentation likely to stop	32	90
Served mulled wines	60	140
Heat treatment for red fruits	80	176
Boiling	100	212

Metric	Imperial
1.25 ml	¼ tsp
2.5 ml	½ tsp
5 ml	1 tsp
15 ml	1 tbsp
300 ml	½ pt (10 fl oz)
550 ml	1 pt (20 fl oz)
4.5 L	1 gal (160 fl oz)
7 g	¼ oz
15 g	½ oz
20 g	¾ oz
25 g	1 oz
50 g	2 oz
75 g	3 oz
115 g	4 oz
225 g	8 oz
300 g	10 oz
350 g	12 oz
450 g	16 oz (1 lb)
1 kg	2 lb 3¼ oz

1 Imperial gal = 6 standard bottles (wines)

Index